THE VIRTUOUS MAN

Breaking The Men's Code

THE VIRTUOUS MAN

Breaking The Men's Code

KEVIN TONEY

K-Tone Enterprises
All Rights Reserved Worldwide

First Edition
10 9 8 7 6 5 4 3 2

Book Cover design by The AIO Corporation

Book Edited by Elle Jai
The Right Connection Entertainment Group©

Text Review/Edit by Richelle and Kirk Taylor

Interior Design by Rudy Milanovich and Keith Leon

Photography by Jeff Lewis

Electronic Book ISBN: 978-0-9840228-1-6
Soft Cover book ISBN: 978-0-9840228-0-9

K-Tone Enterprises
Porter Ranch, CA

THE VIRTUOUS MAN
Breaking The Men's Code

Published by K-Tone Enterprises
19360 Rinaldi Street #476
Porter Ranch, California 91326
website: www.kevintoney.com

Deterring Immorality by Counting It's Cost, The exorbitant price of sexual sin by Randy Alcorn.
Eternal Perspective Ministries, www.epm.org

Family Christian Pledge by Pastor Dudley Rutherford, Shepherd Of The Hills Church, Porter Ranch, California.

The Principles Of Manhood by Ronald M. Barnes. www.ctri2009.com

The Manformation Project… www.manformation.org

Five Things I Wish I'd Known Before Marriage – by Dave Boehi.

100 Answers to 100 Questions About Loving Your Wife – by Lila Empson. Published by Christian Life.

CONTENTS

Part III. Additional Resources

PRELUDE

This book is dedicated to my loving son, Jason.

ACKNOWLEDGENTS

All praise, glory and honor to God, for this writing experience comes from You. Thank You Father for planting a seed in my heart and giving me a vision of how to harvest it. It is solely through Your love, grace, mercy and forgiveness that I stand here today with my wife and family. I would like to thank my wife Phyllis for believing in my greater good and for trusting and believing that I could show God and her something different. You have encouraged me to go deeper with the writing of this book so that not only would I have a better understanding of this journey, but also more importantly that I would be able to clearly share with others what I've learned in the process. I can only thank God for the countless ways you have demonstrated your love for me. For me you are truly the "Virtuous Woman" of which Proverbs chapter 31 speaks of. From Proverbs 31:29, I say to you *"There are many virtuous and capable women in the world, but you surpass them all" (NLT).* Without your deep, rich love and unyielding faith, this book would not have been written.

I would like to acknowledge and thank Dr. Richard Harrison for his excellent and divine counsel to my wife and me. You helped us understand and see what God's love between us was and how to take the steps to restore our marriage. You gave me the time and tools to overcome the most difficult challenge of my life. Without your guidance and wisdom, our marriage would have never survived. Your work with us has been a blessing and has tremendously helped our marriage to now strive and blossom beyond anything we could have imagined! I'd like to thank my friend James Newton for encouraging and directing me to "fight for my family" and to begin seeking God's divine guidance. James you are one of God's angels as you got my attention in a big way! I'm forever grateful to you for being a true friend in my time of despair and need. To Yochanan Marcellino, thank you for your brotherhood, friendship and many suggestions regarding this book. Your vision has been a blessing in my life. I would like to acknowledge Shepherd Of The Hills Church in Porter Ranch, California for presenting good, clear, and inspirational Bible teaching. The yearly themes of worship along with fellowship and study in the men's group have greatly helped to rebuild and reconnect my spiritual foundation. To Marcus Slaton, thanks for the book, Every Man's Battle™, which God used to pierce my heart!

I'd like to thank Keith Leon for his thoughtful suggestions and help in completing this work. You were sent to me from God to give me the finishing touches! To Kirk and Richelle Taylor, you two arose to the meaning of what true friendship means. Thank you for investing in God's kingdom by making yourselves available and so giving of your time regarding the additional editing details of this book. To the Manformation Project™, thank you for letting me be a part of helping to shape our young men's lives using faith-based principles."

INTRODUCTION

It is interesting that we see many examples and results of sexual infidelity and yet men continue to do the same thing. In recent history we've witnessed a president of the United States almost getting impeached, many other high level politicians resigning from office, one of the biggest sports figures of all time getting divorced and losing all credibility, along with many other top entertainers, athletes and celebrities losing their power, fame and fortune all because of sexual infidelity or misconduct. Every one of them has had to pay extraordinary consequences for their behavior. Some on a very public stage and some in private ways. I too am a part of that list of men who willingly risked everything for the thrill of greener pastures outside my marriage. There are many other reasons that marriages break up but infidelity and sexual misconduct is perhaps one of the most foolish yet avoidable causes. Proverbs 6:32 states: *"But the man who commits adultery is an utter fool, for he destroys his own soul."* It is one of the most painful things you can ever do to your wife and family.

This book is a result of me wanting to study God's word regarding marriage, fatherhood and what those commitments mean. It was God's grace and mercy that kept my marriage together when it was at its weakest. It was God's divine appointment that led me to my friend who referred me to the Bible in my hour of greatest need. It was God's words that helped turn my thinking and priorities around when I was lost in a life of sin. I stand here today as a first hand witness for one of God's greatest miracles in my life. Because of my unfaithfulness and foolish behavior, I faced the ultimate scenario: divorce from my wife. By all human and worldly standards, my marriage should have failed and fallen apart like so many others have experienced. Only through God's miracles am I still standing stronger than ever with my wife and family here today. My pastor recently stated that the purpose of a miracle is for God's glory to be revealed, resulting in people putting their trust in him. My experience is a first hand example of what a miracle means in real everyday life. It has resulted in me putting my full trust in God.

However, in order for that to have taken place and remain firmly with me, it required a change of heart and mind. So God got my attention in a very big way and shut me down. In 1 Peter 3:7 it says: *"If you don't treat your wife right, God will not answer your prayers."* This happened, as

I was being unfaithful to my wife. God tried many times to get my attention but in my foolishness and denial, I rejected his appeals. He then cut things off. I would blame not garnering the level of success in my music career that I aspired to on things like luck, people not giving me the proper level of respect, and racism. After all I thought that I had paid my dues, been persistent and had an abundant amount of God-given talent. The record label I was with during that time put out recording after recording, but my career was not progressing as it should have. I knew I was making better recordings and writing music on a very high level, but things were just not moving forward. I fell flat and it never dawned on me that I was responsible for this happening. My continual sinning and mistreatment of my wife was causing God to not answer my prayers and thus bless my paths. My wife has said that God does not reward bad behavior. This was so true with me and I missed this point entirely! God had to shut me down and humble me to get my attention. Work began to thin out and activities came to a halt. I could not "get arrested" in terms of shows and career building opportunities. So I took time away from my career to search and reconnect myself spiritually. I needed time to apply my heart to God's words and teachings. It became clear to me that only God could and did provide the ways and means for this to happen. I am forever grateful for my wife's willingness, cooperation and love to give me the opportunity and time needed to work on those changes.

The "Men's Code," is a mode of conduct and thought which is counter to "God's Code" (the written Word in the Bible) regarding relationships of marriage and family. Through the "Men's Code" men have been taught that it's okay to disrespect women, to treat them only as physical objects of desire, to partially commit to their spouses and to have relationships outside of the marriage. Time after time men choose to follow this code (just as I did) only to eventually face the timeless truth of God's teachings and commands regarding marriage and family. His instructions on how to think and act in these areas should be the basis of our daily living. When we are not in harmony with His teachings and His will for us, we will ultimately suffer far-reaching and often times irreversible consequences.

The book begins by telling the story of how I learned and embraced the "Men's Code," its early beginnings, its rise to power, my crash and my point of turning things around. Then the book becomes a bible manual for men to study God's word on becoming virtuous. This section is organized by topics of God's wisdom and commands I desired to have in my heart, mind and soul. They also directly reflect the issues I struggled with surrendering to and understanding. The verses are in no way a complete listing of all that's written in the Bible regarding this subject matter. The biblical manual section has thirteen chapters with each consisting of a chapter introduction, Bible study verses that relate to each topic, a life application section, a self-study section, and journal section. Study application notes are from the New Living Translation (NLT) unless otherwise indicated as NIV (New International Version). PDR refers to Pastor Dudley Rutherford and PMM refers to Pastor Miles McPherson. Added inspiration came from reading NFL coach Tony Dungy's book "Quiet Strength" where he honors and gives glory to God above everything else in his life. I'm driven by his daily challenge given to his football players… **What have you done today to be a better father and a better husband?"**

In this same spirit, it is my mission to give hope and encouragement to help bring men who have lost their commitment, connection and purpose in their marriages back to their wives and families. I trust that by sharing my failures and victories that men may gain insight, spiritual and practical tools that will better equip them to face the journey of marriage. It is my prayer that this book will inspire men to seek becoming "The Virtuous Man."

In Jesus Name…Amen

April 9, 2011

Part I

My Story

1. **Detroit** *(Early Beginnings)*

My story begins growing up in Detroit, Michigan. I was eight or nine years old and my mother and father had recently separated. Along with my two older brothers and sister we lived with my mother in a small two bedroom upstairs level of a two-story home in a lower middle class neighborhood. For a short time after our parent's separation, we did not have any contact with my father. Several months later this issue eased up somewhat and we were able to have visits with him. I remember one of the first things my father did to reconnect with us was to get his three boys together for a meeting. I had no idea why we were going over to his house, but for some reason my mother had our big sister come along. Once at his house, our sister went down the hall to hang out in one of the bedrooms and then our father began to whisper to us. He quickly and quietly told us that he was going to talk about having sex with a woman. All three of us sat up attentively and listened as our dad tried to verbalize what that all meant. I don't recall any specific instructions on the physical act and what it entailed. But I do remember that it simulated me to want to go out and find some girl to try it with. This was my earliest recollection of getting the "Men's Code" and it came through my father. As I reflect upon that encounter and the information I received, I've realized the following: (1) Sex was a physical activity (2) It was something that was discussed in secret (3) It did not address anything spiritual (4) No discussion or perspective on how to interact with females was given. As we grew older, I don't recall my father ever addressing me nor my brothers on how we should love a woman, what special qualities we should look for and what our behavior and attitudes should be toward women. I'm not blaming my father for how he communicated to us, because that was most likely what he observed from the men in his life growing up. Like many other men, he passed down the "Men's Code" from his generation to us. I should point out that while living with my dad and mother I was baptized at around seven years old at the church around the corner from our house. We would also attend my father's church, Second Baptist Church alternating with our neighborhood church, Community Baptist Church. I don't recall getting any information about what was appropriate and inappropriate regarding sexual behavior from any of those worship services or church related activates. After my parents separated, my siblings and I stopped attending church, and Sundays simply became just another day. It wouldn't be until I was in the tenth grade that I would be in church regularly as a pianist working with my sister who was the music director. By that point, being in church was just a job.

Going back to my mother's house that evening, I remember being somewhat sexually aroused, but didn't quite understand what I was feeling. I was curious and began to think about girls and how I could try what my Dad had spoken to us about. Months later while playing with the kids in the neighborhood, I ran into such an opportunity. I somehow managed to talk a girl around my age to come with me to the alley. It was getting dark outside and kids were starting to go home. We found a secluded spot and tried to have sex. This experience did not work so well because I had no idea what the sexual anatomy of a female was and what I was suppose to do in that situation. My dad did not discuss these details and I left that encounter thinking, " Is that all that there is to this?" I thought that playing army, sports and music was better and more exciting than what I had experienced in the alley. As I reflect on this encounter it brings up other important aspects of the "Men's Code": (1) That men would often pass on incomplete and misguided information about sex to young boys (2) There is no discussion about the consequences of having sex at a young age or getting a woman pregnant and the responsibilities that comes with that (3) There was no discussion of when the right time was to engage in sexual activity. (4) There was no discussion from a spiritual or biblical perspective on what God's word reveals about sexual behavior. By the fifth grade I was receiving further sex education from looking at bikini-clad centerfold girls in Jet Magazine™.

After these early episodes, I began to focus more on music and other fun activities with my friends. As I continued on to Junior High School, I advanced rapidly with music and opportunities to perform began to abound. During this time I played cello, saxophone and piano extremely well and was involved in the top performing ensembles at school and throughout the city. I also became attracted to girls and would walk some home from time to time. There would be occasional supervised weekend visits to some as well. I remember my older brothers dating and having girlfriends during that time. They would dress nicely, comb their hair in cool styles and put on cologne. They would let me hang around them, but there were no talk about girls and how you date them. Today, they are both single, never been married and can't seem to maintain any long-term meaningful relationships with women. I'm sure they have their individual issues with the "Men's Code" as well but, have not been able to address its deeper issues. During this time, there were occasional visits to see my father. But I can't recall any conversations that would have helped me develop maturely into manhood regarding sexual matters or even general life issues. At his home, I remember seeing nude pictures and paintings of women in open view. Perhaps this was his interest in the art form of female anatomy. But I did not take that perspective from such display as it indicated that this is how men lived and viewed women. Here I gleaned additional aspects of the "Men's Code": (1) Men often did not take responsibility to shape and guide their sons in practical living matters (2) It was cool to have images of nude females and to view them mainly from physical perspective. On a positive note, my father would always come to my performances and was very supportive of my music endeavors. By the time I was fourteen I tried to get sex from a girl again. This time I succeeded in knowing what to do physically but got to the point when the orgasm was about to happen and got scared. Not only did I not know what to do at that point, but also I didn't know how to react to the physical and emotional responses that were taking place. I withdrew from the situation and didn't discuss it with anyone. I was embarrassed and sex continued to remain somewhat of a mystery for me. It was fortunate that I didn't go through with the entire act of sexual intercourse; I could have gotten that girl pregnant or caught some disease. A major flaw of the "Men's Code" is that boys and young men often learn critical information by themselves resulting in creating wrong attitudes and behaviors toward women.

My next major encounter with the "Men's Code" took place when I was in high school.

Things were changing and as I continued to advance musically, I was also growing more attracted to girls. I remember being rejected sexually by the first girl I pursued. She was an attractive violin player and I planned a date with her by making arrangements with my piano teacher to use his apartment after our date one evening. Well that didn't work out well and I didn't accomplish my goal with her. I was very disappointed and frustrated with the process and thought it required a lot of time away from music. At age sixteen my hormones were raging and I was feeling that it was time to find out what real sex with a woman was all about. During that time my information relating to sex was coming mostly from fellow male students at school who spoke of their sexual triumphs. All of the 'players' talked about which girls were hot and sexy and how they got it on with them.

My first real sexual experience would come from a prostitute. One day after school I was enroute to my piano teacher's apartment to practice on his grand piano. His apartment was in the downtown area of Detroit, which had a few bars where prostitutes would hang around. Being somewhat naïve, I wasn't aware of what their profession was about but was certainly aroused by seeing them in their seductive clothing. I remember being lured into a bar looking at all those sexy women, but not knowing what to do. It didn't take long for one of them to approach me and ask if I wanted to do anything. Well I acquiesced to her persuasion and thus received my first sexual experience with a woman. I remember the satisfaction I had received and thought that getting sex from a prostitute was easier than having to spend time dating a girl hoping that something would happen. That was the beginning of embracing the "Men's Code" that taught that it was okay to buy sex from a woman and the bigger misconception that love can be bought. In the eleventh grade I got a girlfriend who was more than willing to engage in sexual activity. We had sex just about everywhere we would go. I thought that I had now figured it out somewhat. During my last year of high school, I was performing throughout the city of Detroit with it's best and most prolific musicians. I was receiving additional "Men's Code" information from the older musicians I performed and hung out with. I had the opportunity to observe how these men talked and interacted with their women. However, no one "schooled" me regarding how to respect and love women appropriately. Nor did any of the married musicians talk to me about how to treat your wife properly. I would still occasionally visit the area where prostitutes hung out to have sex with them. This was where I learned to relate and treat women in my early developmental stages. This would be some of the baggage and thinking that I would later bring into my marriage.

2. **Washington, D.C.** *(Crowning Touches)*

After graduating from high school, I moved to Washington, DC to attend Howard University. My first year found me living in Meridian Hill, a co-ed dormitory and there were plenty of beautiful young ladies there. After several attempts of trying to "hit" on some of them, I found myself in similar situations that I'd experienced in Detroit. That was, I hadn't mastered the game of seduction. Because of my strong commitment to mastering music studies, I did not want to invest too much time trying to figure this out. So, I discovered where the "ladies of the night" hung out and would feed my sexual appetite through prostitution from time to time. This approach seemed to work well as it allowed me not to get distracted with chasing after women. Into my second year at college, I began to experience normal sexual relationships with girlfriends.

I came to Howard to study with jazz great Donald Byrd who was the head of the jazz studies department there. Meeting and closely being around him would give me the crowning touches of the "Men's Code." When I arrived at the music department, Donald took me under his wing immediately. I started performing with him, frequently traveling around the country with his jazz band that included seasoned veterans. Many of them were my heroes whom I had heard on various recordings. I was in jazz heaven and would have this close student-teacher-mentor-employer relationship with him for the next seven years. It was during these formative years that I was able to closely observe his relationships with the women in his life and they were as follows: (1) His main lady lived with him in Washington, D.C. (2) He had another woman in New York who took care of certain aspects of his personal business (3) His woman in California managed his music business activities (4) He had another woman in Europe. These key ladies always did things for Donald in some significant way. As I traveled and performed with him I observed that he had women in other cities as well. So the idea that a man could have several women in many places got introduced to me in a big way. Thus I received indoctrination into higher levels of the "Men's Code" by being around someone whose lifestyle was a major influence on me.

By my junior year I became quite well known as a member of 'The Blackbyrds'. This was a select group of music students from Howard University that Byrd put together initially as his back-up band. We began to record albums and had great success, both critically and commercially. As full time students we traveled frequently to record and perform around the country. We also had huge album sales and performed internationally as well. In a short time the band became extremely popular and that opened up a big door for the "Men's Code" to be put to full test. I began to have girls in several cities as I tried to model what I saw from other men in the music and entertainment business. There were some ladies that I liked more than others, but many of them were just good sex exploits. Now I was in the position of having as many women as I wanted. The 'Men's Code" had reached full effect by this time, as I embraced and was living the code's ultimate quest. I had no idea how deeply it had absorbed me! It was like an addiction, as I would go from one woman to the next one. I can remember that my first serious girl friend at college was someone who I didn't do right. There was a time I contacted some minor venereal disease and gave it to her. Embarrassed, I broke the news to her and then we went to the hospital to get it taken care of. The Men's Code does not encourage safe sex, because many men prefer to risk having unprotected sex because it "feels better." The "Men's Code" promotes that being unfaithful is something that is acceptable for men. As the band's career took off to greater heights, we began doing shows with the top artists during that period that ranged from Earth Wind & Fire, Parliament/Funkadelic, Ohio Players to Grover Washington, Herbie Hancock, Kool & The Gang, Richard Pryor and more. The Blackbyrds racked up impressive awards and accolades, which included two Grammy nominations, several RIAA gold record awards, number one group awards from Billboard Magazine and Record World, an NAACP Image Award and more. Then girlfriend number two came along and I really liked her, but continued to engage in outside sexual pursuits. During my last year in college, I began visiting some churches as a few of my musician friends encouraged me to go. But, even with this new interest in going to hear God's word and hearing the great inspirational music, it would take something of greater impact to change my walk.

After graduating from college I had plans to take a trip and visit some women in a few different cities, but that never took place. God had other plans for me as I met my future wife and things began to change. I found myself wanting to spend more and more time with her, and we became best friends. We started off slowly and then things heated up between us and after two years of dating, I asked her to marry me. I knew that I loved this woman in a very special way and thought I was ready to make that commitment. But, I had little idea of what it would take to grow and maintain a marriage. I simply was not mature enough and did not have the proper foundation for what it required. Nothing in the "Men's Code" prepares a man for a long lasting marriage. By that time, I had built up so much personal baggage that I brought some of it into our marriage. Although counseled by our pastor, some of it required much work to overcome. Making the transition from being an artist with a very popular band to a married man didn't happen easily. There were times that I faced temptations during my marriage with some I'd act upon occasionally. Then there was the part of the "Men's Code" that stayed with me that said that if things weren't going well with my wife, I could go find a prostitute and not have to deal with confrontational issues. I would have to learn how to peel off those layers of thinking and behaviors that were so deeply ingrained. As time progressed it was our deep, sincere love for each other and mutual belief in God that would keep us together. Through the ups and downs, the good and bad times, through the raising of our two children and all my shortcomings, we managed to sustain our marriage. I credit my wife's strong faith, courage and persistence in making huge sacrifices that helped our family to grow and stay together. She was the spiritual backbone of our family and came from a much stronger religious background than me. During our marriage we'd go to various churches, but I would listen selectively, putting little effort in applying various marital teachings into practice.

Were there married men in our life that were good models of what a successful marriage looked like? Yes, and one in particular was a man named Harold Turney. He was a hard working man with good virtues and he took very good care of his family and home. He'd give me sound advice on balancing my career and family life. His entire family was close friends to my wife and family. He was someone whom I looked up to and was there to give good counsel in other life areas as well. But there was never a discussion of marriage from a biblical perspective. My other important mentor during this time was Andrew. He was a brilliant musician, good businessman and had a loving and successful marriage. I performed and recorded with Andrew for several years around the same time I was a member of The Blackbyrds in the Washington, DC area. He and his lovely wife were always together whenever we performed and they worked very well together as a team. He was very respectful and loving to his wife and they were an excellent example of how being married and being a musician could work harmoniously. However, I received additional "Men's Code" through him as well. He had a huge collection of pornographic books at his home that were organized by female body parts. So, on times I'd visit him and viewed his collection, I'd become sexually aroused. I want to make it very clear that I'm not blaming Andrew for my response, for I should have not allowed my thoughts to get out of control. By God's standard, anytime a married man looks at a woman with lust in his mind and heart, he is committing a form of adultery. This can be in the form of viewing images or real women with the thought of sexual activity in one's mind. Matthew 5:27-28 states *"You have heard that the law of Moses says, "Do not commit adultery. But I say, anyone who even looks at a woman with lust in his eye has already committed adultery in his heart."* Andrew most likely thought of his collection as art, but nevertheless viewing that type of material could also fill one's mind with inappropriate thoughts.

So the "Men's Code" continued to find subtle ways to infiltrate my married life. There came a time later when I flagrantly disrespected our marriage by buying into the ultimate trap of the "Men's Code." I engaged in a full-fledged affair for nine months. Subsequently my wife found out and confronted me with evidence that I couldn't deny. After twenty-five years of marriage, I hit my lowest point and my world crashed! It took seeing the harm and deep pain that it brought on my wife before I was ready to take the necessary steps to change my walk. But, before that could begin I had to stop being in denial of what had happened and what had led to this critical point in my marriage.

3. Los Angeles *(The Crash)*

I can remember times during the affair that I questioned why I continued to do it. I would say on occasion that I was going to stop but, managed to continue getting more involved. At that time, my family and I were living in Los Angeles, California with both my wife and me fully engaged into the music and entertainment industry. For some reason, I foolishly thought in this big metropolitan city I could maintain and hide an affair from my wife if I kept it at a good distance from home. I can see in retrospect that I was spinning totally out of control in my self-indulgent behavior and had taken on a secret life. Here the "Men's Code" blinded me to the truth that having an extramarital affair at any distance away from your wife is just wrong. There were times I thought about what I would do if I got caught in this situation. Would I leave my family? No way, that never was an option. But, somewhere inside of my out of control world was a part of me that wanted my wife to catch me cheating. I was not a good liar and certainly not thorough in trying to conceal my activities. You might say that I was naïve to think that my wife would not at some point begin to question my frequent disappearances and alibis. The "Men's Code" will have you convinced that you can continue getting away with that kind of behavior and won't get caught as long as you're clever with deception. Again, the "Men's Code" says that it's okay to break your marriage vows and to disrespect your marriage. Through my wife's good detective work and God's will, she was able to confront me with solid evidence of my affair. My first response was to deny her accusations. Then I tried to explain that I was with a prostitute. Here the "Men's Code" was directing me to lie, be deceptive and place blame outside of my responsibility. I had allowed foolishness and buying into the beliefs of the "Men's Code" to almost destroy the most important thing God had given me: my wife and family.

My turning point came after I spoke to my friend James Newton. It was the day after my wife confronted me and asked me to leave our home so that I could give complete thought as to what I was now going to do. At that point I didn't know what to do or who to turn to. There seemed liked there was no way out. I checked into a nearby hotel and woke up the next morning and called James. I told him about my situation and that I had tried to reach him earlier to use him as an alibi. He told me that if I had reached him that he wouldn't have done it. He explained that he too was once in my situation and lost his wife in divorce. He told me that if I loved my wife and family, that I should fight for them and do whatever was necessary to change my predicament. He then directed me to read Bible verses that clearly pointed out the sin of adultery, its consequences and what God directs us to do regarding our marriage (Proverbs Chapter 5, 6, 7 along with other scriptures found in 1 Corinthians). I refer to them again in the chapter on God's Advice and Consequences of Adultery. He then gave me his pastor's telephone number who recommended us to a marriage counselor. This counselor was a believer in God's word and would use moral, practical and biblical references to help heal and restore our marriage. My wife also brought me a Bible titled "Everyman's Bible" that I began to read and study daily. It then became clear that I could only turn to God for help and that there was nothing I could do on my own to resolve it. I knew that God was calling me to remove certain things from my life and now was the time to address them. This was the point I became determined to turn my thoughts and behaviors around and begin walking down the right path. I wanted to find out and know all that God teaches about marriage and being a Godly man. I began writing down Bible scriptures which addressed specific topics that gave instruction and insight into these areas. I wanted to organize by topic the material in the Bible that addresses how men can become virtuous. My wife pointed out that the Bible has no specific chapter that covers being a virtuous man like Proverbs chapter thirty-one covers the attributes of being a virtuous woman.

For the next six years I immersed myself in gaining spiritual enlightenment and renewal. It was like going to school to learn and digest God's teachings. It was during this time that I worked on writing this book. Through this journey, I'm extremely grateful that God provided a way for me to have victory over my sins by: (1) Completely taking me away from the things that were destroying me, (2) Not giving up on me, (3) Sending earthly angels to help me (my wife, our marriage counselor and James), (4) Humbling my heart to receive His help, (5) Giving me His words in the Bible for guidance and inspiration, (6) Allowing me the time to make the necessary changes, (7) Giving me new beginnings in my life.

4. Resurrection *(New Beginnings)*

Although my wife agreed to stay and work together on restoring our marriage, I would have to face the fear of her wanting to divorce several times throughtout this process. I knew that I hurt her pretty badly and that it wasn't going to be easy and would require great patience and faith on her part. But through God's grace, she was willing to do what ever was necessary to help save our marriage. Before me was the task of doing the necessary work to overcome my situation. I would have to experience a season of learning and inner growth that would not come easy. It required every ounce of faith and courage to begin this work on myself. Above all, it required total surrender to God's will, as I knew that victory would only come through God's power. I would wrap my thoughts and heart around Proverbs 3:5 which says: *"Trust in the Lord with all your heart and lean not on your own understanding."* However my practical teaching and application would come from our marriage counselor, Dr. Harrison. He got me to see that from early in my life, I never understood or respected God's purpose of a woman and marriage. He made me realize that my perception of right and wrong had become jaded and inaccurate and that I had willingly accepted sin. He got me to see that I had used music as a vehicle for sin. He also got me to seek the root causes for my behaviors and got me to realize that by the time we married, I'd developed a deeply sinful nature and habits that continued to grow and fester. I remember him telling me that sometimes an apology isn't enough to heal the hurt and wounds caused by such wrong behaviors. He told me to not let what I didn't have overshadow what I do have and that my joy, contentment and success should not be determined by chart position or career successes but, by my relationship with Jesus Christ.

Our counselor did so much to help restore our marriage and put me on the right track of living God's true purpose. We'd meet weekly in a public restaurant instead of his office thus giving us a less formal setting to freely discuss our issues. His guidance included many key elements beginning with both of us agreeing to continue with the sessions and to listen with attentiveness to each other without interfering. He directed us to not bring up old arguments and issues that were not related to what was being discussed in the moment. It was brought up for me to begin speaking up, not allowing unresolved issues to build up and become explosive later. Dr. Harrison got us both to recognize what role we played in our marriage problems. He pointed out that even though I was wrong to have the affair, my wife unknowingly had enabled me to pursue it. During my individual sessions our counselor directed me to revisit my childhood and journal things that I brought as baggage into our marriage. This meant facing child hood occurrences I had not come to terms with and would include: (1) Fears that I receive from growing up in my parents house (2) Rejections from females early in my life and (3) Bad examples from men regarding how to treat women. He then gave me tools to resolve those issues through practicing more effective communication and speaking with those I needed to confront past issues with. He further directed me to deeply reflect on how I'd been so out of control and to address how I had hurt others, disappointed my wife and children and betrayed the trust she'd unconditionally given me. I was asked to confront the issue of why I did not take my vows seriously and that I had fragrantly disrespected my wife, our marriage and God. In our sessions together he also encouraged me to be honest in recognizing what it was that made me seek the affair. To examine what I thought was missing in my marriage and to examine my commitment to my wife over the course of our marriage. Most hard to do for me was the issue of coming totally clean on all the important details of the affair. This took several months of counseling as I seemed to want to selfishly protect myself by slowing giving out this badly needed information little by little. In this area I was directed to give thought to clearing up any questions and examine if there was anything I hadn't said or expressed to my wife.

Of great importance during our sessions was the help given in how I would move forward from this situation and maintain the right attitudes and reactions. Our counselor challenged me to be prepared in what to say when other women try to prey. For example: "That you can't touch or top my wife. She is the best and only woman for me. She is my God-given wife." We discussed what I'd do when inappropriate physical urges arise and how to avoid a relapse of inappropriate behavior using scriptures and positive thoughts. This would include staying away from people, places and things that could trigger old impulses. He then instructed me to make a list of Godly minded men I knew who would encourage righteous thoughts and would hold me accountable to God's standard of conduct for a married man. He encouraged me to find a true male friend who I could share and confide in. During that time, Dr. Harrison became that person for me.

Our counselor was very effective in giving us some practical marriage tools. He got us to recognize the weak and strong points of our personalities and how not to use them to control the other. We needed to begin openly expressing our needs without fear of judgment from the other. I had to relearn how to love, respect and appreciate my wife and begin not taking her for granted at any level. I was encouraged to constantly let my wife know how much I valued her input and conversation and that I deeply missed her when she is away from home working. I shared with our counselor that I had to change my old ways of thinking to include making a priority of spending quality time together and be able to take time away from whatever I was doing at any given moment. I would have to work on making her feel special and to show concern for the little things that mattered to her. Other key issues that came out of our counseling sessions included: (1) For me to practice being a good listener and become a good shoulder for her to cry on (2) To ask my wife what she wanted in our relationship and be willing to do it (3) To re-examine what I wanted in our marriage and to openly discuss this with my wife (4) Establishing better communication through taking walks and doing other fun activities together (5) To study my wife, recognizing her downtime and knowing when the best time to talk is, (6) To work on spontaneity by replacing old routines with new and fresh approaches in the area of intimacy (7) To better connect with my wife's innermost thoughts and make a deeper spiritual and emotional commitment to her.

My next step was to right anyone that I'd wronged as a result of my sin. This meant that I start first with apologies to my wife and children, then to friends and associates who knew my wife and me. My wife requested that I send a letter to those people whom I'd disrespected by bringing the woman I had the affair with around them in public. It was as follows:

June 19, 2005

Dear Friends, Colleagues, and Associates,

After a long year of self-assessment and deep reflection, I am compelled to write this letter to you. In the recent past, many of you witnessed me in the company of a woman other than my wife. She (I mentioned her name) and I were willing participants in an extramarital affair during a period of time in which I was totally self-absorbed. We both knew the circumstances of each other's lives and yet we went forward fully knowing the risks. Some of you have not hesitated in expressing your dismay with my lack of judgment, I am aware that not only did I not respect you, I also didn't respect myself nor my wife and family. I now know that I made you very uncomfortable by bringing this person into your presence. I regret putting you in such a position. This entire ordeal has been the biggest mistake I have made in my life. I have offended and hurt many people that I care deeply for and who care deeply for my wife, my family and me. For that I am profoundly sorry. I am working every day to show you the person I really am. I know that I have tarnished your thoughts but hope that over time you will be able to see that I am forever changed for the better in every aspect of my life.

More importantly, I apologize to you Phyllis. I acknowledge that my behavior was reprehensible. No words can ever speak to the depth of sorrow my heart feels for the pain I have caused you. You have been there for me through every difficult moment in our history together. Even now, you are still standing with me and by me. Your grace and dignity are unshakeable. A lesser woman would have been gone early on. I am making it my life's work to be the man you deserve to have. I will rise to you. This is my promise.

I love you and honor you,

Kevin

5. Coda *(Finishing Touches)*

The finishing touches of embracing "God's Code" would come over time and would manifest itself in several ways. God connected us to two married couples with long lasting marriages that we could be next to and closely observe. Bernard and Shirley have been married for over forty years and do everything together and Bernard always honors his wife with such deep reverence publicly and privately. Their principles of living are based on (1) Luke 12:48 which says *"To whom much is given, much is required and to whom much more is given, much more is required,"* and (2) *"To live a life of no regrets."* Their strong bond of love, faith and giving is contagious and is a great source of inspiration for both my wife and me! They exemplify God's design and purpose of marriage in a beautiful and clear reflection. Then there is Marilyn and Billy, a couple that has been married and working together in the entertainment business for over forty years. Throughout all their tremendous success and traps of the music business, they managed to keep God and family first. Today they continue working together in their ministry "Soldiers For The Second Coming." It is here that God has brought me next to them, performing monthly while being able to observe how they effortlessly and joyfully do God's work together. Through their testimonial ministry they seek the lost giving hope to many by presenting the Gospel message together as man and wife. God put my wife and me next to two outstanding married couples with long marriages that are excellent examples of how a husband and wife can be one, giving glory to God.

God's finishing and continuing touches also began to manifest itself in my work. I composed and recorded a collection of solo piano pieces that I dedicated to God for His blessings in getting us victoriously through our difficulties. This album, entitled "Heart Of Gratitude" (aka "A Grateful Heart") became my life's new soundtrack and I began a season of performing this music at various churches and spiritual centers. Guest performances at The Trinity Broadcast Network's Praise The Lord program, Saddleback Church, Seattle Center For Spiritual Living, Las Vegas Center for Spiritual Living, Guidance Church and other spiritual venues responded positively to my new calling. Scoring music for film, writing music books and teaching at a Los Angeles College were additional blessings that the Lord opened up for me as well. Then there is *The Manformation Project* in which I am a mentor to young boys. It is a Los Angeles-based rites of passage setting that brings boys ages ten to eighteen into contact with Godly minded men to cultivate positive growth. It is interesting to note that now, most of my income is now derived from faith-based and community based sources. My wife and I also started *The Toney Family Foundation*, focusing on arts and music related philanthropy. I began experiencing working positively and lovingly with my wife in many new and exciting ways. Most importantly, my wife and I spent quality time praying and worshiping together.

Prior to our marriage counseling sessions, I never had anyone talk to me in depth about the virtues of marriage from a Godly prospective exactly what God required from man and wife and His instructions on how to achieve it. At my church there were several sermons that the pastor preached on marital fidelity which were excellent in content. But it would take attending the two-day "The Art Of Marriage" seminar at my church for me to receive the total package. Here the many aspects of marriage were presented in a clear and practical manner. Finally after thirty-one years of marriage, I was getting the finishing touches of "God's Code" right at my neighborhood church. It was one of the most awesome, eye-opening and heart-touching learning experiences I've ever had! Major teachings include:

1. Understanding that the ultimate purpose of marriage is to reflect God's glory. In this area the seminar gives great insight on marriage being a covenant and not a contract. It also speaks on the importance of marriage vows and breaks down what a traditional vow really means.

2. Recognizing that marriage is not about you but, about going through life together serving God and each other. Here it points out the importance of what this commitment means, along with understanding the process of husband and wife becoming one. Several tips are given on how a man can nourish and cherish his wife as well.

3. The importance of praying together and building a spiritual foundation with your wife and family. Some of the tools given include praying daily with your wife, reading the scriptures together and praying together with your children.

4. Accepting that God calls men to sacrificially love and lead their wife. In this area the seminar defines biblical role of husbands as found in Ephesians 5:25 - 33 which says: **Husbands**, *love your wives, as Christ loved the church and gave Himself up for her, (33) Let each one of you love his wife as himself, and let the wife see that she respects her husband.* It then defines the biblical role of the wives as found in Ephesians 5:22-24 that reads: **Wives**, *submit to your own husbands, as to the Lord. (23) For the husband is the head of the wife, even as Christ is the head of the church, His body, and is Himself its Savior. (24) Now as the church submits to Christ, so also wives should submit in everything to their husband.*

5. Tips on communication and how to focus on addressing one issue at a time when a conflict arises. James 1:19 is a great illustration on what to strive for. It says:*" My dear brothers and sisters, take note of this, everyone should be quick to listen, slow to speak and slow to become angry..."*

6. Insights on what to do when love begins to fade and how to rekindle romance back into a marriage.

7. Steps to seeking and granting forgiveness and tips on handling conflicts in your marriage,

8. God's design for sex and effective ways of communicating about sex to your spouse. The seminar brought out that oneness before God, pleasure and procreation are the three reasons the Bible gives for sexual intercourse in marriage.

9. Ideas on helping your marriage last a lifetime, which includes loving and staying committed to each other, each spouse recognizing the need for God in their marriage and trusting that God gives grace and direction as you trust Him.

10. Leaving a Godly legacy of love for future generations by recognizing that one of the greatest gifts we can give is faithfulness and fidelity in marriage.

For further information visit: www.TheArtofMarriage.com

Concluding Thoughts

With these tools I am now better equipped in my marriage to reflect God's purpose and design. I now have stronger insight and wisdom to make the right decisions and actions in my marriage and family life. I now fully understand and accept my role as husband. It is with a heart of gratitude that I humbly give all glory and honor to God! Now my work is to continue digesting and applying these teachings on a daily basis and to share my work with others. I'm now in graduate school seeking my master's degree in loving my wife based on God's word and promises. I've come full circle from my early beginnings of embracing the "Men's Code" to receiving and joyfully applying "God's Code." Just as God has given me a new season for new beginnings, He will do the same for you in your quest to become the "Virtuous Man." The following chapters are the spiritual tools I used to help make significant life changes and can serve as a biblical manual for men.

Part II

His Story, His Glory

6. Understanding What Love Is

When I got married to my wife, I knew I was in love with her and deeply desired to please her. I knew I wanted to spend my life with her and to raise a family. I knew we would have to communicate and grow together along the path of our marriage. But I didn't understand what love was. I felt love from within and from my wife, but didn't understand that love was always right with and in front of me with the beautiful wife God had given me. I didn't understand that love was always within me and around me through God's grace and mercy, Jesus Christ's great sacrifice and the Holy Spirit. I didn't realize that love required tremendous patience and forgiveness and not wanting things to always go my way. I didn't understand that real love required a strong unwavering commitment, something that was unselfish and not self–centered. *1 Corinthians 13:4-5 says, "Love is patient and kind. Love is not jealous or boastful or proud or rude. Love does not demand its own way. Love is not irritable, and it keeps no record of when it has been wronged."* This is what I would need to learn and put into practice with my marriage. After more than twenty years of marriage I was inwardly fighting the "Men's Code." This is the code of conduct that teaches men how to relate to and treat women. This is taught to most men at a very early age when they are boys and can observe older boys and men living by it. It is taught either in direct terms through men telling young boys and men how to treat females in this manner, or indirectly by young boys and men observing those older boys and men living out loud the "Men's Code." It starts by teaching men that love is self-centered and self-satisfying. It starts by teaching little boys that females are physical objects of gratification and that they should be judged mostly by their physical attractiveness. It misleads boys to think that they can buy the love of a female through physical gifts and not by forming a spiritual, Godly connection with them. As little boys grow and develop into men, so does the "Men's Code" grow within their minds affecting their thoughts and deeds in negative and damaging ways. I let the "Men's Code" consume and distort my view and understanding of what love is. There would come a point in my journey that I would have to seek "God's Code" to break the "Men's Code", that time would come after twenty five years of marriage, my wife discovered that I was committing adultery. I had to decide immediately and quickly that I loved her and my family deeply enough to want to stop my behavior and to try to work through the situation. This is when it became clear to me that I needed to embrace "God's Code" (which is the written word of the Bible) with a sincere and humble heart if there was ever to be hope for our marriage to withstand what was now before us.

I didn't understand that the healing needed after such hurt would require much painful time to rebuild trust, faith and love back into our relationship. I now understand that through "God's Code", that love is the most important thread of our lives. It's what can heal, restore and keep our marriages from faltering and is the fuel that makes them keep growing. I had to learn to see and understand God's love from my wife. I now understand why God puts us next to others. I didn't realize that my wife and family was a gold mine and that they couldn't be topped by anything or anyone. They were the best that God had to offer to me. I didn't understand what an awesome woman she was and that she always deserved the very best from me. Love is never to be taken for granted by any of us.

1 Corinthians 13:8 say that *"There are three things that will endure, faith, hope and love and the greatest of these is love."* (NIV) The following scriptures help me to understand and have a new understanding of what love is and what love isn't.

Bible Study-Chapter 6

1 *Corinthians 13:4-13* (4) Love is patient and kind. Love is not jealous or boastful or proud (5) or rude. Love does not demand its own way. Love is not irritable, and it keeps no record of when it has been wronged. (6) It is never glad about injustice but rejoices whenever the truth wins out. (7) Love never gives up, never loses faith, is always hopeful, and endures through every circumstance. (8) Love will last forever... (13) There are three things that will endure faith, hope and love, and the greatest of these is love.

Romans 12:9-1 Don't just pretend that you love others, really love them. Hate what is wrong. Stand on the side of good. (10) Love each other with genuine affection, and take delight in honoring each other.

1 *Peter 4:8*, Most important of all, continue to show deep love for each other, for love covers a multitude of sins.

1 *John 4:7-10, 16-17* (7) Dear Friends, let us continue to love one another, for love comes from God. Anyone who loves is born of God and knows God. (8) But anyone who does not love does not know God, for God is love. (9) God showed how much he loved us by sending his only son into this world so that we may have eternal life through him. (10) this is real love…(16)… God is love and all who live in love live in God, and God lives in them. 17) And if we live in God, our love grows more perfect…

Song Of Songs 4 (*Young man speaking romantically of his bride*) (1) How beautiful you are, my beloved, how beautiful! Your eyes behind your veil are like doves. Your hair falls in waves, like a flock of goats frisking down the slopes of Gilead. (2) Your teeth are as white as sheep, newly shown and washed. They are perfectly matched, not one is missing. (3) Your lips are like a ribbon of scarlet. Oh how beautiful your mouth! Your cheeks behind your veil are like pomegranate halves, lovely and delicious. (4) Your neck is as stately as the tower of David, jeweled with the shields of a thousand heroes. (5) Your breast are like twin fawns of a gazelle, feeding among the lilies. (6) Before the dawn comes and the shadows flee away, I will go to the mountain of myrrh and to the hill of frankincense. (7) You are so beautiful, my beloved, so perfect in every part. (8) Come with me from Lebanon my bride. Come down, from the top of Mount Amana, from Mount Senir and Mount Hermon, where lions have their dens panthers prowl. (9) You have ravished my heart, my treasure, my bride! I am overcome by one glance of your eyes, by a single bead of your necklace. (10) How sweet is your love, my treasure, my bride! How much better it is than wine! Your perfume is more fragrant than the richest of spices. (11) Your lips my bride, are as sweet as honey. Yes honey and crème under your tongue. The scent of your clothing is like that of the mountains and the cedars of Lebanon. (12) You are like a private garden, my treasure my bride! You are like a spring that no one else can drink from, a fountain of my own. (13) You are like a lovely orchard bearing precious fruit, with the rarest of perfumes. (14) nard and saffron, calamus and cinnamon, myrrh and aloes, perfume from every incense tree, and every other lovely spice. (15) You are a garden fountain, a well of living water, as refreshing as the streams from the Lebanon mountain.

Song Of Songs 5:9-16 (*Young woman speaking romantically of her groom*)…(9) O woman of rare beauty, what is it about your loved one that brings you to tell us this. (10) My lover is dark and dazzling, better than ten thousand others! (11) his head is the finest gold, and his hair is wavy and black. (12) His eyes are like doves beside brooks of water; they are set like jewels. (13) His cheeks are like sweetly scented beds of spices. His lips are like perfume lilies. His breath is like myrrh. (14) His arms are like round bars of gold, set with chrysolite. His body is like bright ivory, aglow with sapphires. (15) His legs are like pillars of marble set in sockets of the finest gold, strong as the cedars of Lebanon. None can rival him. (16) His mouth is altogether sweet; he is lovely in every way. Such, O woman of Jerusalem, is my lover, my friend"

Song Of Songs 7 *(Young man speaking)* (1) "How beautiful are your sandaled feet, O queenly maiden. Your rounded thighs are like jewels, the work of a skilled craftsman. (2) Your navel is as delicious as a goblet filled with wine. Your belly is lovely, like a heap of wheat set about with lilies. (3) Your breast are like twin fawns of a gazelle. (4) Your neck is as stately as an ivory tower. Your eyes are like the sparkling pools in Hesbon by the gate of Bath-rabbim. Your nose is as fine as the tower of Lebanon overlooking Damascus. (5) Your head is as majestic as Mount Carmel, and the sheen of your hair radiates royalty. A king is held captive in your queenly tresses. (6) Oh how delightful you are, my beloved, how pleasant for utter delight! (7) You are tall and slim like a palm tree, and your breast are like it's clusters of dates. (8) I said I will climb up into the palm tree and take hold of its branches. Now may your breast be as grape clusters, and the scent of your breast like apples. (9) May your kisses be as exciting as the best wine. Smooth and sweet, flowing gently over lips and teeth... *Young Woman*....(10) "I am my lover's, the one who he desires. (11) Come my love, let us go out into the fields and spend the night among the wildflowers. (12) Let us get up early and go out into the vineyards. Let us see whether the vines have budded, whether the blossoms have opened, and whether the pomegranates are in flower. And there I will give you my love. (13) There the mandrakes give forth their fragrance, and the rarest fruits are at our doors, the new as well as the old, for I have stored them up for you, my lover."

Song Of Songs 8:6-7 (6) Place me like a seal over your heart, or like a seal on your arm. For love is as strong as death, and its jealousy is as enduring as the grave. Love flashes like fire, the brightest kind of flame. (7) Many waters cannot quench love; neither can rivers drown it.

If a man tried to buy love with everything he owned, his offer would be utterly despised.

John 13:34 "So now I am giving you a new commandment. Love each other, just as I have loved you, you should love each other.

Study Application Notes

1 *Corinthians 13:4-7* In marriage, our love must be unselfish and exude all of the descriptions that Paul list. He also defines love as a commitment to act in certain ways toward others. And further, we must never confuse love for lust. It is possible to practice this kind of love with our spouses and others only if God helps us put aside our own desires and instincts, so that we can give love without expecting nothing in return. Love is the greatest of human qualities, and is an attribute to God himself (1 John 4:8).

13:13 Expressing unselfish love to our spouse and others is evidence that we care. Faith is the content and foundation of God's message, hope is the attitude and focus, and love is the action. When faith and hope are in line, you are free to love completely because you understand how God loves you.

Romans 12:9-10 We are called to let love govern. We are called to love even those we consider to be our enemies. We have all been wronged by others. God's love allows us to forgive them and seek reconciliation. All of us have hurt others. Love requires us to swallow our pride, admit our mistakes, and make that special effort to reach out to those we've wronged. It urges us to make up for the trouble and pain we have caused. Our relationships can then be healed and our own spiritual condition improved.

1 *John 4:7-10* Everyone believes love is important, but love is usually thought of as a feeling. In reality, love is a choice and an action. As I Corinthians 13:4-7 shows, God is the source of our love. He loved us enough to sacrifice his son for us. Jesus is our example of what it means to love because everything He did in life and death was supremely loving. The Holy Spirit gives us the power to love; He lives in our hearts and makes us more and more like Christ. John says, "God is love" not "Love is God." Our world has turned these words around and contaminated our understanding of love. The world thinks that love is what makes a person feel good and that it's all right to sacrifice moral principles and others rights in order to obtain such "love." But, that isn't real love, it is the exact opposite. Selflessness "real love" is like God who is holy, just and perfect. As we grow to be more like him, we grow in our ability to love our spouse and others.

6-17 John spoke again about the importance of love. True Christianity is characterized by loving relationships in which there is no fear. Experiencing such relationships, first with God then with our spouse and other believers is at the heart of spiritual renewal. Mature Christian love delights in helping others and it creates an environment in which we can develop accountability and a new sense of responsibility toward our spouse, others and ourselves.

Song Of Songs 4 (1-7) This intense, private and intimate exchange between a man and a woman speaks of the ecstasy of their love. They praise each other using beautiful imagery. Their intense feelings of love and admiration are universal. Communicating love and expressing admiration in both word and actions can enhance every marriage. (15) Solomon's bride was as refreshing to him as a fountain. Could your spouse say the same about you? Sometimes the familiarity that comes with that comes with marriage causes us to forget the overwhelming feelings of love and refreshment we shared at the beginning. Many marriages could use a course in "refreshing" Do you refresh your spouse, or are you a burden of complaints, sorrows and problems? Partners in marriage should continually work at refreshing each other by an encouraging word, an unexpected gift, a change of pace, a surprise call or note, or even a withholding the discussion of the problem until the proper time. Your spouse needs you to be a haven of refreshment because the rest of the world usually isn't.

Observation: Today's media preaches that immorality and extramarital affairs mean freedom, perversion is natural and lasting commitment is old fashioned. Love has turned into lust, giving into getting, and lasting commitment into "no strings attached." In reality, sexual intercourse, the physical and emotional union of male and female, should be a Holy means of celebrating love, producing children and experiencing pleasure, protected by the commitment of marriage. God thinks sex is important (he created it in Eden), and Scripture contains numerous guidelines for its use and misuse. Sex is always mentioned in the context of a loving relationship between husband and wife.

To highlight this is Song of Songs, the intimate story of a man and a woman, their love, courtship and marriage. The entire book of Song of Songs features the love dialogue between a simple Jewish maiden (the Shalamite woman) and her lover (Solomon the king). They describe in intimate detail their feelings for each other.

Song Of Songs 5:9-16 The young women of Jerusalem force the young bride to remind herself of all that she loved about her husband. Her description begins with his physical attributes, it concluded with her calling him both her lover and friend. (5:16) In a healthy marriage, lovers are also good friends. Too often people are driven into marriage by the exciting feelings of love and passion before they take time to develop a deep friendship. This involves listening, sharing and showing understanding for the others likes and dislikes.

Song Of Songs 7:1-9 Solomon's praise of his bride continues. As the couple matures in their love, the passion did not diminish. Even though marriages may have periods of indifference and rejection, passionate love can last as a marriage grows. Maintaining our marriage relationship is vital to our spiritual growth (10-13) As our love matures, there should be more love and freedom between marriage partners. Here the woman takes the initiative in lovemaking. The security of true love gives both marriage partners the freedom to initiate acts of love and express their true feelings. The couple returned to the countryside to renew their love. They celebrated their renewal in the same place that they met, in the vineyards. This would have reminded them of the tender moments they shared when they first met, when they fell in love. Let this example inspire us to do what we can to put some sparkle and romance back into our marriage.

Song Of Songs 8:6-7 In this final description of love, the woman includes some of its significant characteristics. Love is as strong as death, it cannot be killed by time or disaster, and it cannot be bought for any price because it is freely given. Love is priceless, and even the richest king (Solomon) cannot buy it. Love must be accepted as a gift from God and then shared by the guidelines God provides. Accept the love of your spouse as God's gift and strive to make your love a reflection of the perfect love that comes from God himself.

John 13:34 This Christ like love is to love others (including our spouses) based on Jesus' sacrificial love for us. Jesus was a living example of God's love, as we are to be living examples of Jesus' love. Love is more than simply warm feelings, it is an attitude that reveals itself in action. How can we love others as Jesus loved us? By helping when it's not convenient, by giving when it hurts, by devoting energy to others welfare rather than just your own, by absorbing hurt from others without complaining or fighting back. This kind of love is hard to do. That is why it is noticed so much by others when you do it and they know you are empowered by a supernatural source.

Self Reflection

1. How does this topic apply to me?

2. What truths in this area do I recognize and how can I fully address them?

3. What Bible verses here best encourage and inspire me to want to be a better husband, and spouse this area?

4. What steps can I begin to take today to strengthen myself in this area?

5. Who can I reach out to for personal help and support in this area? (This could be a family member, friend, professional counselor, a spiritual leader or someone you worship with)

Journal

Journal

7. God's Instructions On Marriage

When my wife and I got married we met with our minister several times. Many things were brought up and discussed that were highly important to the foundation of our marriage. Out of those meetings came our vows that we mutually created. But, even with this Godly preparation from our minister, I had no idea that it would take much, much more to grow and sustain our marriage. Reflecting on that period, I see that the "Men's Code" had already made an impact on my thinking in selfish ways. Even in the beginning of our marriage I did not want to change certain attitudes I'd developed. Perhaps if I had grown up solidly learning biblical scriptures and principles of marriage I would have been given the spiritual tools to better embrace marital responsibilities. Even in pre-marriage counseling our minister did not delve into these biblical scriptures regarding marriage. Maybe he assumed I knew them or that my wife who was coming from a much stronger biblical background knew them well.

My insight now is the importance of instructing young boys with these Godly values before they become sexually interested. This will provide them with the spiritual and practical tools to have a healthy, morally strong outlook on marriage. "God's Code" for understanding what marriage is about should not only be taught in Church but reinforced in the home by parents. God's instructions on marriage are clear and don't require a Ph.D to understand. If I had reviewed them periodically, been open to being around Godly married men and been obedient to God's word, perhaps I would have avoided the pitfalls of becoming unfaithful in my marriage. However, in going through this, I now understand that God has a purpose and season for everything that we go through in life. It is in this light that I acknowledge that God used my worst mistakes to allow me the opportunity to begin giving praise, honor and glory to Him alone. He can do this for any of us who are humble enough to want to begin listening to Him! Ephesians 5:33 reads *"Each one of you also must love his wife as he loves himself, and the wife must respect her husband."* Along the way in my marriage journey, I began to fail in this area which resulted in my wife losing respect for me. I've learned that we must nurture and maintain love and respect in our marriages on a daily basis. After closely facing divorce I discovered that only continued study and application of God's written Word would keep me with the right thoughts and actions regarding marriage. After seeing a marriage counselor for two years, I realized that marriages need regular tune-ups just like our automobiles. Attitudes, actions, thoughts, habits, behaviors and how we relate, respond and love our spouses must over time be reviewed and adjusted.

When your marriage is in trouble don't wait until it's too late, ask and seek help. There is no shame in seeking help for maintaining or restoring your marriage. Don't attempt to do this on your own. You will need the wisdom, guidance and experience of someone trained to help you put everything back together. In counseling, it was brought out that I had certain personal baggage from my childhood that I brought into the marriage. The counseling sessions helped me to not only recognize them, but gave me the tools to effectively deal with and resolve them in a way that would no longer be a burden on our marriage. As a child I was never taught by anyone how to treat the woman I would marry. My father and mother were not able to communicate with me or my brothers effectively on this subject. As a teenager and young adult, most of my heroes and role models were not good examples in this area. They showed through their actions and conversations that it was okay to mistreat, disrespect and dishonor your marriage when convenient. They often spoke of women in derogative terms This was what the "Men's Code" taught us at an early age. This is not to say that God didn't show me other positive examples of marriage. I chose somehow to embrace those negative role models because their actions appeared to be the cool thing to do. Today, I'm grateful that God has shown me and put me next to several strong, endearing, Godly married men. I realize that one has to be open and receptive to whom God places next to us in our lives. Those who bring His blessings and positive light into our lives. I thank God for those Godly couples in our life today and use them as examples on how to treat my wife by God's standard. A recent guest minister (Pastor Phillip Wagner) at my Church (Shepherd Of the Hills) gave some excellent advice on what to do when we face challenges or crisis in our marriages. (1) Don't give up, no matter how bad the circumstance or situation may be, (2) Pray for each other and pray with each other, (3) Help build faith in your marriage, (4) Invest in a book or CD that could be helpful, (5) Spend time with couples who have faith and have the kind of marriage that you want. The following verses give a clear understanding of what God expects for both man and woman in marriage. Whenever I see myself being selfish, inattentive or unloving I can quickly read these verses and know what I need to adjust in my thinking and actions.

Bible Study-Chapter 7

Genesis 1:27-28 So God created people in his own image, God patterned them after himself, male and female he created them. (28) God blessed them and told them, "Multiply and fill the earth and subdue it. Be masters of over the fish, and birds and all the animals"

Genesis 2:18-25 (*Marriage is God's idea*) key verses include (18) And the Lord God said, "It is not good for the man to be alone. I will make a companion who will help him. (21) So the Lord God caused Adam to fall into a deep sleep. He took one of Adam's rib and closed up the place from which he had taken it. (22) Then the Lord God made a woman from the rib and brought her to Adam. (23) 'At last" Adam exclaimed. "She is part of my own flesh and bone! She will be called a woman, because she was taken out of a man. (24) This explains why a man leaves his father and mother and is joined to his wife, and the two are united into one. (25) Now, although Adam and his wife were both naked, neither of them felt any shame.

Deuteronomy 24:5 A newly married man must not be drafted into the army or given other special responsibilities. He must be free to be at home for one year, bringing happiness to the wife he has married.

Ephesians 4:2 Be humble and gentle. Be patient with each other, making allowances for each other's faults.

Ephesians 5:21-33 (21) And further, you will submit to one another out of reverence for Christ. (22) You wives will submit to your husbands as you do to the Lord. (23) For the husband is the head of his wife as Christ is the head of his body, the church; he gave his life to be her savior. (24) As the Church submits to Christ, so you wives must submit to your husbands in everything. (25) And you husbands must love your wives with the same love Christ showed the church. He gave up his life for her. (26) to make her holy and clean, washed by baptism and God's word. (27) He did this to present her to himself as a glorious church without a spot, or wrinkle or any other blemish. Instead she will be holy and without fault. (28) In the same way, husbands ought to love their wives as they love their own bodies. For a man is actually loving himself when he loves his wife. (29) No one hates his own body but lovingly cares for it, just as Christ cares for his body, which is the church. (30) And we are his body. (31) As the Scriptures say, "A man leaves his father and mother and is joined to his wife, and the two are united into one." (32) This is a great mystery, but is an illustration of the way Christ and the church are one. (33) So again I say, each man must love his wife as he loves himself, and the wife must respect her husband.

Colossians 3:19 And you husbands must love your wives and never treat them harshly.

Hebrews 13-4 Give honor to marriage, and remain faithful to one another in marriage. God will surely judge people who are immoral and those who commit adultery.

Ephesians 4:26-27 And don't sin by letting anger gain control over you. Don't let the sun go down while you are still angry, (27) for anger gives a mighty foothold to the devil.

2 *Corinthians* 6:14-15 *(Husbands and Wives as Spiritual Partners)*… Don't team up with those who are unbelievers. How can goodness be a partner to wickedness? How can light live with darkness? (15) What harmony can there be between Christ and the Devil? How can a believer be a partner with an unbeliever?

1 *Corinthians* 7 *Key verses include the following* (2) But because there is so much sexual immorality, each man should have his own wife, and each woman should have her own husband. (3) The husband should not deprive his wife of sexual intimacy, which is her right as a married woman, nor should the wife deprive her husband. (4) The wife gives authority over her husband, and the husband gives authority over his body to his wife. (5) So do not deprive each other of sexual relations. The only exception to this rule would be the agreement of both husband and wife to refrain from sexual intimacy for a limited time, so they can give themselves more completely to prayer. Afterward they should come together again so that Satan won't be able to tempt them because of their lack of self control. (6) This is only my suggestion. It is not meant to be an absolute rule. (10) A wife must not leave her husband. (11) But if she does leave him, let her remain single or else go back to him. And the husband must not leave his wife. (12) If a Christian man has a wife who is an unbeliever and she is willing to continue living with him, he must not leave her. (13) And if a Christian woman has a husband who is an unbeliever, and he is willing to continue living with her, she must not leave him. (14) For the Christian wife brings holiness to her marriage, and the Christian husband brings holiness to his marriage. Otherwise your children would not have a Godly influence, but now they are set apart for him. (15) But if the husband or wife insist on leaving, let them go. In such cases the Christian husband or wife is not required to stay with them. (16) You wives must remember that your husbands might be converted because of you. And you husbands must remember that your wives might be converted because of you. (39) A wife is married to her husband as long as he lives. If the husband dies, she is free to marry whomever she wishes, but this must be a marriage acceptable to the Lord.

1 *Peter 3:1-7* *key verses include* (3) Don't be concerned about the outward beauty that depends on fancy hairstyles, expensive jewelry, or beautiful clothes. (4) You should be known for the beauty that comes from within, the unfading beauty of a gentle and quiet spirit. (7) In the same way, you husbands must give honor to your wives. Treat her with understanding as you live together. She may be weaker than you are, but she is your equal partner in God's gift of new life. If you don't treat her as you should, your prayers will not be answered.

Proverbs 19:14 Parents can provide their sons with an inheritance of houses and wealth, but only the Lord can give an understanding wife.

21:19 It is better to live alone in the dessert than with a crabby, complaining wife.

27:15 A nagging wife is as annoying as the constant dripping on a rainy day. (16), Trying to stop her complaints is like trying to stop the wind or hold something with greased hands.

Proverbs 17:9 Love prospers when a fault is forgiven, but dwelling on it separates close friends. (NLT)

Exodus 20:14 *The Ten Commandments state*…#8: Do not commit adultery.

Study Application Notes

Genesis 1:27-28 God made both man and woman in his own image. Neither man nor woman is made more in the image of God than the other. From the beginning the Bible places both man and woman at the pinnacle of God's creation. Neither sex is exalted and neither is diminished. (NLT)

Genesis 1:27-28 God made man/groom in his image and with a specific purpose to carry out God's will. God's instructions were to be fruitful, increase in number, fill the earth and rule over every living creation on earth. God created the woman/bride as the compatible marriage companion to man/groom. (PMM)

Genesis 1:28 The groom/bride marriage is a life giving union. (PMM)

Genesis 2:15-22 Adam and Eve's story reveal the following important points, (1) God defines work for man in the Garden of Eden and also sets consequences for not obeying his commands, (2) God creates woman to be man's helper illustrating that man could not do God's work alone. (3) Using God's manual (the Bible) will greatly help us to live correctly as man and wife. (PMM)

Genesis 2:23-25 A Groom/Bride marriage is compatible with God. This is why kids usually run to their mothers in times of despair because they carried them for nine months. Man and woman were created by God to become one flesh and to fulfill God's plan. We reflect the image of God on earth. The devil wants to destroy this image because he hates God. (PMM)

Genesis 2:24 The Groom/bride relationship, like salvation, is a shameless one-flesh union. The consequences of not living like this are: (1) sexually transmitted diseases, (2) reputations destroyed and heartbreak, (3) being inappropriately attached to somebody you're not supposed to be with, (4) "putting sand in the gas tank" (going against God's design of what marriage is), (5) a warped concept of marriage, relationships, family, sex and self image. (PMM)

Genesis 2:18-25 God's creative work was not complete until he made woman. He could have made her from the dust of the ground, as he made man. God chose however, to make her from the man's flesh and bone. In doing so, He illustrated for us that in marriage, man and women symbolically become one flesh. This is a mystical union of the couple's hearts and lives. Throughout the Bible, God treats this special partnership seriously. If you are married or planning to be married, are you willing to make the commitment that makes the two of you one? The goal in marriage should be oneness. (NIV)

Genesis 2:25 Genesis 2:25 to: Adam and Eve were not embarrassed in their innocence, but after Adam and Eve sinned, shame and awkwardness followed, creating barriers between themselves and God. We often experience these same barriers in marriage. Ideally a husband and wife would have no barriers in marriage, feeling no embarrassment in exposing themselves to each other or to God.

Deuteronomy 24:5 Recently married couples were to remain together their first year. This was to avoid placing an excessive burden upon a new unproven relationship and to give it a chance to mature and strengthen before confronting it with numerous responsibilities. A gardener starts a tiny seed in a small pot and allows it to take root before planting it in the field. Let your marriage grow strong by protecting your relationship from too many pressures and distractions especially in the beginning. We should not expect or demand so much from newlyweds so that they have adequate time and energy to establish their marriage.

Ephesians 4:2 Paul challenges us to live lives worthy of the calling we have received. In our marriage calling, this includes being humble, gentle, patient, understanding and peaceful. No one is ever going to be perfect here on earth, so we must accept and love our spouses in spite of their faults. When we see faults, actions or personalities that annoys us, we should pray for our spouse. Then do even more: spend time together and see if you can, in a gentle and loving way share your feelings and relate to each other regarding those issues.

Ephesians 5:21-33 In a marriage relationship both husband and wife are called to submit. For the wife, this means willingly following her husband's leadership in Christ. For the husband, it means putting aside his own interest in order to care for her as Christ does the church.

Each should be concerned for the happiness of the other. The apostle Paul counseled believers in his day to submit to each other by choice: wives to husbands and husbands to wives.

Ephesians 5:22-31 A Groom-Bride marriage is compatible with salvation. Man represents Jesus and the woman represents the Church (wife-church, husband-Jesus.... Christ/Groom, Church/bride). The wife submits to husband and husband submits to wife. The devil wants to destroy the oneness that God created. (PMM)

Hebrews 13-4 Here we have some practical commands for faithfulness in our marriage. This faithfulness is based on God's empowerment and protection. If we are uncertain which behaviors and attitudes are acceptable, God's clear standards can be a great help. Real love and honor produces tangible actions including respect for your marriage vows, contentment with your spouse, empathy and fidelity. This is a big part of the practice of "rightful living."

2 Corinthians 6:14-15 Paul urges believers not to form binding relationships with nonbelievers, because this might weaken their Christian commitment, integrity or standards. It would be a mismatch. Paul wants believers to be active in their witness for Christ to nonbelievers, but they should not lock themselves into personal or business relationships that could cause them to compromise their faith. Believers should do everything in their power to avoid situations that could force them to divide their loyalty. This thinking holds equally true for married couples as well as for individuals.

1 Corinthians 7:2-5 Marriage is the place for sexual expression and fulfillment. Our bodies don't belong to us, they belong to God. But here, Paul is saying that they also belong to our spouses. If we seek sexual fulfillment outside of marriage, we will find ourselves in a trap of selfish pleasure seeking. If we belong to God and our spouses, we have the potential to act in ways to bring them great joy. Our challenge is to not seek only our personal gratification. As we keep our sexuality within the bounds of marriage, we can discover the joy that comes from living faithfully with another person and before God.

1 Corinthians 7:10-15 Many of us have been hurt by divorce, either as participants or as children of divorced parents. Paul began his words on the subject with a firm reminder of God's command not to divorce. Yet he recognizes that there are situations in which divorce is a legitimate option. The principle that comes from the command and supports Paul's suggestions is found here: (1) God wants us to live in harmony with one another. (2) When we are not experiencing harmony, we need to examine our lives to see if there is anything we can do to change. (3) If after making appropriate changes, we still face significant problems, we may need to help our spouses go through a similar process. (4) Often a marriage counselor is needed to facilitate this process. (5) Divorce is an option only when one of the partners refuses to remain faithful to his or her marriage commitment.

Colossians 3:19 Christian marriage involves mutual submission, subordinating our personal desires for the good of the loved one, and submitting ourselves to Christ as Lord.

1 *Peter 3:1-7* (Verse 1 and 5 is not referenced here because it can often be abused and misunderstood.) Its proper context is in relationship to Roman law in Peter's days were husband and father had absolute authority over all members of his household, including his wife. Peter expressed that wives should show their husbands the kind of self-giving love that Christ showed the church. By being exemplary wives, they could please husbands who were non-believers while still maintaining their rights as free women in Christ. Ideally submission is mutual (Submit to one another out of reverence for Christ- (Ephesians-5: 21)

3:3 We should not be obsessed with fashion, but neither should we be so uncomfortable that we do not bother to care for ourselves. Hygiene, neatness and grooming are important, but even more important are a person's attitude and inner spirit. True beauty begins inside.

3:7 When Peter calls woman the "weaker" partner, he does not imply moral or intellectual inferiority, but he is regarding women's physical limitations. Women today are still vulnerable to criminal attack and family abuse. And the vast majority of our country's poor are single women and their children. A man who honors his wife as a member of the weaker sex will protect, respect, help and stay with her. He will not expect her to work full time outside the home and full time in the home, he will lighten her load whenever and wherever he can. He will be sensitive to her needs, and will relate to her with courtesy, consideration, insight, tact and love.

3:7 If a man is not considerate and respectful to his wife, his prayers will be hindered, because a living relationship with God depends on right relationships with others. If a man misuses his position to mistreat his wife, his relationship with God will suffer.

Proverbs 27:15 (This verse can also apply to husbands) Quarrelsome nagging, a steady stream of unwanted advice, is a form of torture. People nag because they think they're not getting through, but nagging hinders communication rather than helping. When tempted to engage in this destructive habit, stop and examine your motives. Are you more concerned with yourself getting your way, being right, than about the other person you are pretending to help? If you are truly concerned about the other person, think of a more effective way to get through to them. Surprise them with words of patience and love, and see what happens.

Proverbs 17:9 We should be willing to forgive others sins against us. Try not to bring up anything in an argument that's unrelated to the topic in discussion. Strive to acquire God's ability to forget the confessed sins of the past. (NIV)

Exodus 20:14 One of God's most important commandments that deal with our relationship to our spouse. It speaks directly to us all and needs no further explanation.

Self Reflection

1. How does this topic apply to me?

2. What truths in this area do I recognize and how can I fully address them?

3. What Bible verses here best encourage and inspire me to want to be a better husband, and a better man in this area?

4. What steps can I begin to take today to strengthen myself in this area?

5. Who can I reach out to for personal help and support in this area? (This could be a family member, friend, professional counselor, a spiritual leader or someone you worship with)

Journal

Journal

8. Being A Good Husband

What I knew about being a good husband was pretty typical stuff. Things like taking care of our children, paying our bills, having a roof over our heads, providing food and clothing, were things I did with delight. I was pretty good at letting my wife know where and how to get in touch with me in my day-to-day work and travels. We shared good conversation most times and I always felt that she was a loving and inspiring presence in my life. Nonetheless, there were other things that I took for granted regarding her. I was often too selfish with spending quality time with her and was quite often putting my work before her. I would also take her time for granted by often being late for important events and not communicating effectively when I needed to. The Bible tells us in Ephesians 5:25 *"And your husbands ought to love their wives with the same love Christ showed the church."* That means loving, providing and protecting her at all times by putting her emotional and physical needs above your own. The "Men's Code" taught me to view this differently. It encourages men to seek their own satisfaction and gratification first, which put my wife and family in second place. It would manifest itself in such simple ways such as me impulsively buying things I didn't need for myself. On a larger scale and at a more devastating level, it manifested itself in my unfaithfulness to my wife. Being a good husband requires self-control from impulsive behaviors. Trusting in each other to remain sexually pure is a major part of the glue that holds a marriage together. I thank God, my wife and those who helped turn my thoughts and behaviors toward God's ways. For any husband struggling in this area, sexual purity is a habit that can be obtained and maintained through living God's principles as revealed in the Bible. I've learned that honoring your wife and marriage is something you do on a daily, ongoing basis.

I admire those men who show love and honor to their wives in the way they speak about them to others. By how they lift up their strengths, accomplishments and value unselfishly to others. I have also learned that it's not just lip service, but it's loving and honoring our wives by the little things we do and not to seek credit for them. Things like finding out their life goals and taking the time and effort to help fulfill them. Observing and talking to men who have had long, loving and successful marriages will show us much of what we should be doing in our marriage. We should always strive to remain loving, honest and caring to our wife. They will get you through the best and the worst of times. Lastly, but most importantly trust and have faith in the Lord that He will guide you when you just don't know what to do as a husband. God will guide us through all of our challenges if we seek Him first in all our family endeavors.

A very helpful and practical book for men to read is '**100 Answers to 100 Questions About Loving Your Wife**' tm, by Lila Empson. I picked up this book in my church's bookstore and it is a very easy read. It is filled with "take action" things to help improve your relationship with your wife. Topics that resonate with me are: (1) What does your wife long to hear from you and what should be the three most important words in your vocabulary with your wife. "I Love You" it says can never be overused, (2) It gives tips on how to resolve conflicts without creating bigger problems and the importance of praying together before discussing big issues, (3) How to teach your children to speak to their mother and some practical steps you can take to reinforce this, (4) The importance of knowing why and when you should say "I'm sorry" to your wife, (5) Thoughts and tips on how you can show your wife that she's special, (6) How you can learn to work together as a team and that good teamwork consist of good communication, (7) A discussion on what attitudes and behaviors build a foundation for physical intimacy, (8) A look at what love and good listening skills have in common and tips on being a good listener, and (9) The big question of how you can help your wife heal when you've hurt her. This topic particularly hits home with me regarding my hurt to my wife which is cover in detail in this writing. Lila Empson's book further points out that when the hurt is something grievous, an apology is the first step. But most important is a changed, new and improved you! She reminds us that healing takes time and we should allow our wife as much time as she needs to get through this process. What follows are God's instructions on being a good husband.

Bible Study-Chapter 8

a) Value your wife: ***Genesis 2:18, 21-24***, God chose to make woman from the man's flesh and bones. In doing so, he illustrated that in marriage man and woman symbolically become one flesh. And the Lord said, " It is not good for the man to be alone. I will make a companion who will help him." (21) So the Lord God caused Adam to fall into a deep sleep. He took one of Adam's ribs and closed up the place from which he had taken it. (22) Then the Lord God made a woman from the rib and brought her to Adam. (23) 'At last!' Adam exclaimed. " She is part of my own flesh and bone! She will be called 'woman' because she was taken out of a man." (24) This explains why a man leaves his father and mother and is joined to his wife, and the two are united into one.

b) Love like Christ: *Ephesians 5:25* And you husbands must love your wives with the same love Christ showed the church.

(c) Loving your wife: *Ephesians 5:28* In the same way, husbands ought to love their wives as they love their own bodies. For a man is actually loving himself when he loves his wife.

(d) Be faithful to your wife: *Proverbs 5:15-17* Drink water from your own well share your love only with your wife. (16) Why spill the water of your springs in public, having sex with just anyone? (17) You should reserve it for yourselves. Don't share it with strangers.

(e) Honor your wife and marriage: *Hebrews 13:4* Give honor to marriage and remain faithful to one another in marriage. God will surely judge people who are immoral and those who commit adultery

(f) Enjoy your wife: *Ecclesiastes 9:9* Live happily with the woman you love through all of the meaningless days and life God has given you in this world. The wife God gives you is your reward for all of your earthly toil.

Proverbs 5:18-19, Let your wife be a fountain of blessing for you. Rejoice in the wife of your youth. (19) She is a loving doe, a graceful deer. Let her breast satisfy you always. May you always be captivated by her love.

Genesis 2:15-17 The Lord placed the man in the Garden of Eden to tend and care for it. (16) But the Lord God gave him this warning; " You may freely eat any fruit in the garden (17) except fruit from the tree of knowledge of good and evil. If you eat of its fruit, you will surely die.

Thank God For Your Wife

Proverbs 12:4 A worthy wife is her husbands joy and crown; a shameful wife saps his strength.

Proverbs 18:22 The man who finds a wife finds a treasure and receives favor from the Lord

Proverbs 31:10-30 Key verses include; (10) who can find a virtuous and capable wife? She is worth more than precious rubies. (11) Her husband can trust her, and she will greatly enrich his life. (12) she will not hinder him but will help him all her life. (13) She finds wool and flax and busily spins it. (14) she is like a merchant's ship; she brings her food from afar. (15) She gets up before dawn to prepare breakfast for her household and plan the day's work for the servant girls. (16) She goes out to inspect a field and buys it; with her earnings she plants a vineyard. (17) She is energetic and strong, a hard worker. (18) She watches for bargains; her lights burn late into the night. (19) Her hands are busy spinning thread, her fingers twisting fiber. (20) She extends a helping hand to the poor and opens her arms to the needy (21) She has no fear of winter for her household because all of them have warm clothes. (22) She quilts her own bedspreads. She dresses like royalty in gowns of finest cloth. (24) She makes belted linen garments and sashes to sell to the merchants. (25) She is clothed with strength and dignity, and she laughs with no fear of the future. (26) When she speaks, her words are wise, and kindness is the rule when she gives instruction. (27) She carefully watches all that goes on in her household and does not have to bear the consequences of laziness. (28) Her children stand and bless her. Her husband praises her: (29) "There are many virtuous and capable women in the world, but you surpass them all"! (30) Charm is deceptive and beauty does not last; but a women who fears the Lord will be greatly praised. (31) Reward her for all she has done. Let her deeds publicly declare her praise.

Study Application Notes

Genesis 2:18, 21-24 God chose to make woman from the man's flesh and bones. In doing so, he illustrated for us that in marriage man and woman symbolically become one flesh. This is a mystical union of the couple's hearts and lives. If you are married or planning to be married, are you willing to keep the commitment that makes the two of you one? The goal in marriage should be more than friendship, it should be oneness. **2:24** God gave marriage as a gift to Adam and Eve. They were created perfect for one another. Marriage was instituted by God and has three basic aspects (1) the man leaves his parents, and in a public act, promises himself to his wife; (2) the man and the woman are joined together by taking care of each other's welfare and by loving the mate above all others; (3) the two become one flesh in the intimacy and commitment of sexual union that is reserved for marriage. Strong marriages include all three of these aspects.

Ephesians 5:25 How should a man love his wife like Christ loved the church? (1) He should be willing to sacrifice everything for her. (2) He should make her well being of primary importance. (3) He should care for her as he cares for his own body. (NIV)

Proverbs 5:15-17 "Drink water from your own well" is a picture of faithfulness in marriage. It means to enjoy the spouse God has given you. In desert lands, water is precious, and a well is a family's most important possession. In Old Testament times, it was considered a crime to steal water from someone else's well, just like it was a crime to have intercourse with another man's wife. In both cases the offender is endangering the health and security of the family. This passage also urges couples to look to each other for lifelong satisfaction and companionship. God designed marriage and sanctified it, and only in this covenant relationship can we find real love and fulfillment. Don't let God's best for you be wasted on the illusion of greener pastures somewhere else.

Ecclesiastes 9:9 Accept your wife as a gift from God and appreciate the enjoyment and companionship God has given you.

Proverbs 5:18-19 God does not intend faithfulness in marriage to be boring, lifeless, pleasure less, and dull. Sex is a gift God gives to married people for their mutual enjoyment. Real happiness comes when we decide to find pleasure in the relationship God has given or will give us and to commit ourselves to making it pleasurable for our spouse. The real danger is in doubting that God knows and cares for us. We then may resent his timing and carelessly pursue sexual pleasure without his blessing.

Proverbs 18:22 This verse states that it is good to be married. God created marriage for our enjoyment and he pronounced it good.

Genesis 2:15-17 God gave Adam responsibility for the garden and told him not to eat from the tree of knowledge of good and evil. Rather than physically preventing him from eating, God gave Adam a choice and thus the possibility of choosing wrongly. God still gives us choices, and we too often choose wrongly. These wrong choices may cause us pain, but they can help us learn and grow and make better choices in the future. Living with the consequences of our choices teaches us to think and choose more carefully.

Proverbs 31:10-30 Some woman compare themselves to the wife in this chapter and feel inadequate. Actually the women in Proverbs 31 represents a description of the ideal wife. No man should ever expect his wife to completely measure up to these standards. These verses should serve as inspiration for our wives to strive for. Here we see the model of a virtuous and noble wife who excels at practical skills. She is an excellent wife and mother along with being a manufacturer, importer, manager, realtor, farmer, seamstress, costumer, lawyer, doctor, teacher merchant, minister, musician, artist, athlete any other worthy profession! She is trustworthy and helps here husband and children in everything they do. She greatly enriches their married life. She's a sharp businesswoman who works hard and knows a bargain when she sees one and uses her skills to make her family happy and healthy. She cares for her family's physical needs, but she also cares about those outside her home. Extending compassion to those less fortunate than she is. And all the while she has the internal character that her children and husband praise, strength, dignity, wisdom and a sense of humor. These verses remind us to reward our wives for all that they do for our children and ourselves.

Self Reflection

1. How does this topic apply to me?

2. What truths in this area apply to me and how can I fully address them?

3. What Bible verses here best encourage and inspire me to want to be a better husband, father and a better man in this area?

4. What steps can I begin to take today to strengthen myself in this area?

5. Who can I reach out to for personal help and support in this area? (This could be a family member, friend, professional counselor, a spiritual leader or someone you worship with)

Journal

Journal

9. Being A Good Father

I've learned in my thirty years of marriage that being a good father is much more than providing the basics. There is more to parenting than providing food, clothing, and shelter, keeping them healthy and in school. Early on I was concerned with these "basics" as well as spiritual essentials for my children including the basics of teaching God's truths, wisdom and the foundation of faith as revealed in the Bible. I didn't provide the spiritual instruction and foundation to my children as head of our family as directed by God. Oftentimes I did not take them to church or take the time to read the Bible to them. They were spiritually under-nourished! We always prayed at dinner but I did not know how to be that example of a Godly father to them through my daily walk. It wasn't that I was a bad or absent dad, I was uncommitted to God and His Word during my early fatherhood and was not consciously helping to develop them spiritually. By the time I began to renew my connection with God and His word, my son was an adult and my daughter was in her last year of high school.

I'm extremely blessed that our children have turned out to be outstanding adults with good hearts and strong character. Thank God that my wife through her early spiritual grounding was able to be that example of a Godly woman to our children. As adults, I'm learning to allow them seek their individual relationships and understanding of God at their own pace and level. I now try to show them by example what it is to be a Godly, loving father. I look for opportunities to share my insight and spiritual growth as situations arise with reference to biblical scripture in conversation that they can apply to daily living. In trying to heal past hurts and misunderstandings, I humbly explain to my children my flawed decisions without excuse and in total honesty. Proverbs 22:6 states *"Teach your children to choose the right path, and when they are older, they will remain upon it."* Proverbs 13:24 states, *"If you refuse to discipline your children, it proves you don't love them. If you love your children, you will be prompt to discipline them."* It is our responsibility to teach our children to know the difference between making right and wrong choices. I now understand how important it is to teach and inspire strong biblical discipline to your children by giving them the tools they'll need to live fruitful Godly lives. Fruits that they can pass on to their children. It is my hope that my children will teach their children God's Word and His ways at an early age. I also know that it is my mission to pass on God's word and teachings to children in need everywhere.

My pastor preached a sermon titled "Desperate Parenting" in which he stated "The most important thing you can do for your child is to follow Christ with all your heart. The second most important thing to do is to follow the instructions found in Ephesians 5:21-33" (This scripture text is found in Chapter 2 Bible Study section). In order to be Godly fathers we must first work at becoming Godly husbands. He also offered this advice about disciplining our children, to do it with love and take the following steps: (1) Tell them why (2) Make sure they understand (3) Spank them (4) Hold them telling them that it was done to teach and love them (5) Tell them why again 6) Make sure they understand again by asking them to tell you why they received their punishment. May the following Bible verses inspire you to instruct your children in God's word and teachings. *"*

Bible Study-Chapter 9

Balancing Responsibility, Love and Discipline

Proverbs 13:24 If you refuse to discipline your children, it proves you don't love them. If you love your children, you will be prompt to discipline them.

Ephesians 6:4 And now a word to you fathers, don't make your children angry by the way you treat them. Rather, bring them up with the discipline and instruction approved by the Lord.

Colossians 3:21 Fathers, don't aggravate your children. If you do, they will become discourage and quit trying.

1 *Kings 2:2-3 (David talking to his son, Solomon)* (2) " I am going where everyone on earth must someday go." Take courage and be a man. (3) Observe the requirements of the Lord your God and follow all his ways. Keep each of the laws, commands, regulations and stipulations written in the book of Moses so that you will be successful in all you do and wherever you go.

1 *Timothy* 5:8 But those who don't care for their own relatives, especially those living in the same household, have denied what we believe. Such people are worse than unbelievers.

Teach using God's word and be an example

***Deuteronomy* 6:4-9** (4) "Hear, O Israel! The Lord is our God, the Lord alone. (5) And you must love the Lord your God with all your heart, all your soul, and all your strength. (6) And you must commit yourselves wholeheartedly to these commands I am giving you today. (7) Repeat them again and again to your children. Talk about them when you are at home and when you are away on a journey, when you are lying down and when you are getting up again. (8) Tie them to your hands as a reminder, and wear them on your forehead. (9) Write them on the doorposts of your house and on your gates."

***Psalms* 78:4-7** (4) We will not hide these truths from our children but will tell the next generation about the glorious deeds of the Lord. We will tell of his mighty power and miracles he did. (5) For he issued his decree to Jacob, he gave his law to Israel. He commanded our ancestors to teach them to their children, (6) so the next generation might know them, even the children not yet born that they in turn might teach their children. (7) So each generation can set its hope anew on God, remembering his glorious miracles and obeying his commands.

***Proverbs* 1:8** Listen my child, to what your father teaches you. Don't neglect your mothers teaching.

Use God As Model Father To Follow

***Psalms* 103:13** The Lord is like a father to his children, tender compassionate to those who fear him.

***Proverbs* 3:11-12** My child don't ignore it when the Lord disciplines you, and don't be discourage when he corrects you. (12) For the Lord corrects those he loves, just as a father corrects a child in whom he delights.

***Matthew* 7:9-11** You parents, if your children ask for a loaf of bread, do you give them a stone instead? (10) Or if they ask for a fish, do you give them a snake? Of course not! (11) If you sinful people know how to give good gifts to your children, how much more will your Heavenly Father give good gifts to those who ask him?

James 1:18 In his goodness he chose to make us his own children by giving us his true word. And we, out of all creation, became his choice possession.

Your Reward

Proverbs 22:6 Teach your children to choose the right path, and when they are older, they will remain upon it.

Hebrews 12:9-11 (9) Since we respect our earthly fathers who disciplined us, should we not all the more cheerfully submit to the discipline of our heavenly Father and live forever? (10) For our earthly fathers discipline us for a few years, doing the best they know how. But God's discipline is always right and good for us because it means we will share in his holiness. (11) No discipline is enjoyable while it is happening, it is painful! But afterward there will be a quiet harvest of right living for those who are trained in this way,

Disciplining Your Child

Proverbs 13:24 It is not easy for a loving parent to discipline a child, but it is necessary. The greatest responsibilities that God gives a parent are the nurture and guidance of their children. Lack of discipline puts parents' love in question because it shows lack of concern for the character development of their children. Disciplining children averts long-term disasters. Without correction, children grow up with no clear understanding of right and wrong and with little direction in their lives. Don't be afraid to discipline your children. It is an act of love!

Proverbs 29:15 The rod of correction imparts wisdom, but a child left to himself disgraces his mother.

Proverbs 23:13 Do not withhold discipline from a child, if you punish him with the rod, he will not die.

Proverbs 23:14 Punish him with the rod and save his soul from death

Titus 2:6-8 Similarly, encourage the young men to be self–controlled. (7) In everything set them an example by doing what is good. In your teaching show integrity, seriousness and soundness of speech that cannot be condemned, so that those who oppose you may be ashamed because they have nothing bad to say about us.

Study Application Notes

Proverbs 13:24 It is not easy for a loving parent to discipline a child, but it is necessary. The greatest responsibility that God gives a parent is the nurture and guidance of their children. Lack of discipline puts parents love in question because it shows lack of concern for the character development of their children. Disciplining children averts long-term disaster. Without correction, children grow up with no clear understanding of right and wrong and with little direction in their lives. Don't be afraid to discipline your children. It is an act of love!

Ephesians 6:4 The purpose of parental discipline is to help children grow, not to provoke them to anger or discouragement. Parenting is not easy; it takes lots of patience to raise children in a loving, Christ-honoring manner. Frustration and anger should not be the cause for discipline. Instead, parents should act in love, treating their children as Jesus treats the people he loves. This is vital to children's development and to understanding of what Christ is like.

Colossians 3:21 Children must be handled with care. They need firm discipline administrated in love. Don't alienate them by nagging, deriding or destroying their self-respect so that they lose heart.

1 Kings 2:2-3 David instructed his son Solomon how to rule and whom to trust. David advised his son to keep his eyes on God. As parents, we need to sit down and talk with our children just as David did with Solomon. This will increase our children's respect for us and equip them to face the challenges ahead.

1 Timothy 5:8 Family relationships are so important in God's eyes. The Apostle Paul says that a person who neglects his or her familial responsibilities has denied the faith. Are you doing your part to meet the needs of those in your immediate family and those in your family circle?

Deuteronomy 6:4-9 This passage sets a pattern that helps us relate the word of God to our daily lives. We are to love God, think constantly about his commandments, teach the commandments to our children and live each day by the guidelines in his word. We are told specifically to share God's wisdom with our children. Here we are reminded to pass on the blessings of God's word by not only teaching it, but through our lifestyles as well.

Psalms 78:4-7 God commanded that the stories of his mighty acts and his laws be passed on from parents to children. This shows the purpose and importance of religious education, to help each generation obey God and set their hopes on him and not the things of the world. It is important to keep children from repeating the same mistakes as their parents and ancestors. What are you doing to pass on the history of God's work to your children and the next generation?

Proverbs 1:8 Our actions speak louder than our words. This is especially true in the home. Children learn values, morals and priorities by observing how their parents act and react every day. If parents exhibit a deep reverence for and dependence on God, the children will catch these attitudes. Let them see your reverence for God. Teach them right living by giving worship an important place in your family life and by reading the Bible together.

Psalms 103:13 In the same manner that a loving father cares about his children, God has compassion and concern on all who call on him. God's love never ceases, trust him.

Proverbs 3:11-12 Discipline means to "teach and train" Discipline sounds negative to many people because some disciplinarians are not loving. God however is the source of all love. He doesn't punish us because he enjoys inflicting pain, because he is deeply concerned about our development. He knows that in order for us to become morally strong and good, we must learn the difference between right and wrong. We should model our loving discipline to our children along these Godly premises.

Matthew 7:9-11 Christ is showing us the heart of God the Father. God is not selfish, begrudging, stingy or thoughtless. He is a loving father who understands, cares and comforts. Let us men use these Godly traits to model fatherly thoughts and actions with our children.

James 1:18 Like God gave mankind (his children) his true word (the Bible) we as fathers should give that same word to our children daily and make them, along with our wives our most choice possession.

Proverbs 22:6 A parent's ultimate goal is to train his or her child to lead a Godly life. If children learn to respect authority, love others, and obey God while they are young, there is a good chance they will stay on that path when they are older. Teach and train your children to choose the right way.

Proverbs 23:13-14 Some fear that they may forfeit their relationship with their children if the discipline them and that their children will resent them for it. Correction won't kill children and it may prevent them from foolish moves that will.

Hebrews 12:9-11 Who loves his child more, the father who allows the child to do what will harm him, or the one who corrects, trains and even punishes the child to help him or her learn what is right? It's never pleasant to be corrected or disciplined by God, but his discipline is a sign of his deep love for us. When God corrects you, see it as proof of his love and ask him what he is trying to teach us. We may also respond to discipline in several ways: (1) we can accept it with resignation; (2) we can accept it with self pity, thinking we don't really deserve it; (3) we can be angry and resentful to God; (4) we can accept it gratefully as the appropriate response we owe a loving Father.

Titus 2:6 This advice given to young men was very important. In ancient Greek society, the role of the husband/father was not viewed as a nurturing role, but merely as a functional one. Many young men today have been raised in families were fathers have neglected their responsibilities to their wives and children. Husbands and fathers who are examples of Christian living are important role models for young men who need to see how it is done.

Titus 2:7-8 Paul urged Titus to be a good example to those around him so that others might see Titus's good deeds and imitate him. If you want someone to act a certain way, be sure that you live that way yourself. Then you will earn the right to be heard, and your life will reinforce what you teach. As parents we can be a good example to our children so that they can see our good deeds and imitate them also.

Self Reflection

1. How does this topic apply to me?

2. What truths in this area can I recognize and fully address them?

3. What Bible verses here best encourage and inspire me to want to be a better father in this area?

4. What steps can I begin to take today to strengthen myself in this area?

5. Who can I reach out to for personal help and support in this area? (This could be a family member, friend, professional counselor, a spiritual leader or someone you worship with.)

Journal

Journal

10. Divorce

1 Corinthians 7:28 state that... *"But those who marry will face many troubles in this life"*...(NIV). Divorce is a very scary thing and no one gets married thinking about it. One of my biggest troubles hit after being married for 25 years as I found myself facing the real possibility of divorce. In the Bible, Malachi 2:14-15 (NIV) it states *"But you have been disloyal to her, though she remained your faithful companion, the wife of your marriage vows."* Then it goes on further and asks the question *"Didn't the Lord make you one with your wife? In body and spirit."* Because of my disloyalty and subsequent affair, my wife had the right to seek and pursue divorce. I had fallen into the ultimate "Men's Code" booby trap. I bought into the attitude of (1) it's okay to have an extra-marital affair as long as no one knows or finds out about it (2) it's okay to take your time and resources away from your wife and family and give them to a stranger, (3) it's okay for you to engage in risky behavior that could not only have serious consequences for you but, also for your wife and family, (4) it's okay to think selfishly about sexual pleasure that's totally inappropriate and without any reverence for God and his consequences for such behavior. The "Men's Code" also encourages us to let our pride get in the way, to not man up and take full responsibility for our actions. It says we should place blame on our wives and others for our behaviors. It teaches men that it's okay to abandon our marriage and family when the storms are most fierce. I had to remember that I was the one who took the action; neither my wife nor anyone else made me do it! Even though our situation was extremely difficult, God miraculously saved and restored our marriage. He did this in such a way that it was clear that this victory was only possible through God's love and power alone. Neither my wife nor I could ever take credit. God began to work to soften and open both our hearts to hear what His will was for us. He then directed our steps in making it possible to put our marriage and life back together.

When faced with having to make a choice between continuing to live a life of sin or fighting to save my family, I chose to fight. I had to fight against all the misconceptions and attitudes I had about women and why I thought I could continue to act with such bad behavior. This behavior greatly hurt my wife and family and I was determined to change my steps. It was the advice of a Godly friend whom I shared my situation with that he immediately referred me to read Bible Scriptures, Proverbs Chapters

5,6 and 7. (These Scriptures deal with adultery and how to avoid falling into the sin) as well as Ephesians 5:22-32 (scriptures dealing with wives and husbands). He shared with me that he had a similar experience with his marriage but was unsuccessful at avoiding divorce. He told me that if I loved my wife and family, then stand and fight for them! This helped to begin the process of opening my heart and moving pride out of the way to hear the word of God regarding adultery and marriage. This same friend referred us to a spiritual based marriage and family counselor. Next to our faith, seeing and sticking with our counselor was the most important aspect of our healing and restoration. For a period of one year we had group and individual sessions and for an additional year I continued counseling sessions on an individual basis. This kind of commitment from me to our marriage gave me an opportunity to show my wife something completely different about me. We could not have achieved this by ourselves and needed the professional and spiritual guidance that the counselor was able to abundantly supply. God had sent his angels to my rescue, to bring me back from the land of the lost and become one of God's returned sheep. I knew then that God was working actively and in full measure in my life. His presence was everywhere and in clear view. I was now willing to be open to do whatever it took to make positive changes in my life through God's power and strength. If any of you are facing divorce or other major marital problems, seek God first and then find a marriage counselor who has a strong spiritual walk and principles. If neither of us didn't commit to consistent and long term counseling, our marriage would have never recovered.

It was my wife's strong faith, belief and love of God that greatly encouraged me to seek the painful truth. That is gaining a clear realization of how and why my thinking led me away from our marriage vows. She also encouraged and enlightened me that we could take and make this walk of faith in God to restore what we had worked on for over twenty-five years! It is to God's glory and honor that we can today be an example to others whose marriages had failed or are in similar trouble that real and genuine change and healing could come about in the midst of a storm. It was truly God's will that delivered us from divorce and allowed our marriage to survive and strive once again. Our marriage and life is in many ways much better and stronger than it was in our early years. 1 Corinthians 7:13 say *"And if a Christian woman has a husband who is an unbeliever, and he is willing to continue living with her, she must not leave him."* It goes on to say in verse (16) *"You wives must remember that your husbands might be converted because of you. And you husbands must remember that your wives might be converted because of you."* I believe that this applied to me even though I was baptized at an early age because I later lived away from God's word in some areas of my life. My wife's faith and belief helped win me back to wanting to live life through God's words and teachings. By all accounts to Biblical Scripture, my wife and I should have been divorced; she would have had every right from a spiritual and legal perspective to do so. I applaud my wife, who when faced with knowing that she could have easily divorced me based on my actions and behaviors, chose to listen to God's voice. The voice that said: I will renew and transform your marriage if you will walk in faith and put your trust in Me. Proverbs 3:5 says *"Trust in the Lord with all your heart and lean not on your own understanding."* This is what we both surrendered to in order to receive God's healing in our marriage. Our pastor summed up the practical steps that are needed to keep marriages from faltering. Marriage Savers: (1) Study the Scriptures, (2) Christian counseling, (3) Faithful to church, (4) Prayer and prayer, (5) Invite God to work on you, wait for God to work on your spouse. (PDR) These steps are what worked for my marriage and is the model I continue to use for daily maintenance."

Bible Study-Chapter 10

Malachi 2:14-16 You cry out, "Why has the Lord abandoned us? I'll tell you why! Because the Lord witnessed the vows you and your wife made to each other on your wedding day when you were young. But you have been disloyal to her, though she remained your faithful companion, the wife of your marriage vows. (15) Didn't the Lord make you one with your wife? In body and spirit you are his. And what does he want? Godly children from your union. So guard yourself; remain loyal to the wife of your youth. (16) "For I hate divorce," says the Lord, the God of Israel. "It is as cruel as putting on a victim's bloodstained coat." Says the Lord almighty. "So guard yourself; always remain loyal to your wife"

Deuteronomy 24:1-4 (1) Suppose a man marries a woman but later discovers something about her that is shameful. So he writes her a letter of divorce, gives it to her, and sends her on her way. (2) If she then leaves and marries another man, (3) and the second husband also divorces her or dies, (4) the former husband may not marry her again, for she has been defiled. That would be detestable to the Lord.

Jesus' discussion about Divorce and Marriage

Matthew 5:31-32 (Jesus speaking) "You have heard the law of Moses says, 'A man can divorce his wife by merely giving her a letter of divorce.' (32) But I say that a man who divorces his wife, unless she has been unfaithful, causes her to commit adultery. And anyone who marries a divorced woman commits adultery."

Matthew 19:3-9 (3) Some Pharisees came and tried to trap him (Jesus) with this question: "Should a man be allowed to divorce his wife for any reason?" (4) "Haven't you read the Scriptures? Jesus replied. They record that from the beginning God made them male and female. (5) And he said, 'This explains why a man leaves his father and mother and is joined to his wife, and the two are united as one.' (6) Since they are no longer two but one, let no one separate them, for God has joined them together (7). "Then why did Moses say a man could merely write an official letter of divorce and send her away?" they asked. (8) Jesus replied, "Moses permitted divorce as a concession to your hard-hearted wickedness, but it was not what God had originally intended. (9) And I tell you this; a man who divorces his wife and marries another commits adultery, unless his wife has been unfaithful." (See Mark 10:2-12)

Mark 10:11-12 "Whoever divorces his wife and marries someone else commits adultery against her. (12) And if a woman divorces her husband and remarries, she commits adultery."

Luke 16:18 "Anyone who divorces his wife and marries someone else commits adultery, and anyone who marries a divorced woman commits adultery."

1 Corinthians 7:28 ...But those who marry will face many troubles in this life...(NIV)

1 Corinthians 7:10-11 Now, for those of you who are married I have a command that comes not from me, but from the Lord. A wife must not leave her husband. (11) But if she does leave him, let her remain single or else go back to him. And the husband must not leave his wife.

1 *Corinthians* *7:12-17* (12) If a Christian man has a wife who is an unbeliever and she is willing to continue living with him, he must not leave her. (13) And if a Christian woman has a husband who is an unbeliever, and he is willing to continue living with her, she must not leave him. (14) For the Christian wife brings holiness to her marriage, and the Christian husband brings holiness to his marriage. Otherwise your children would not have a Godly influence, but now they are set apart for him. (15) But if the husband or wife insist on leaving, let them go. In such cases the Christian husband or wife is not required to stay with them. (16) You wives must remember that your husbands might be converted because of you. And you husbands must remember that your wives might be converted because of you. (17) You must except whatever situation the Lord put you in, and continue on as you were when God first called you…

1 *Corinthians* *7:27-28* Paul's *wisdom* (27) If you have a wife, do not end the marriage. If you do not have a wife, do not get married. (28) But if you do get married, it is not a sin. And if a young woman marries, it is not a sin.

Study Application Notes

Malachi 2:14-15 Divorce in those times was exclusively practiced by men. They broke faith with their wives and ignored the bonding between a husband and a wife that God instilled (the two become one person), as well as his purpose for them (raising children who know and love the Lord "Godly offspring"). God hates divorce. He intended family commitments to be binding. Some of us may have experienced firsthand the pain of a broken marriage. A broken family is a serious hindrance to spiritual growth. We need strong relationships to hold us accountable and keep us on the right track.

2:15-16 Guard yourself means to have the same commitment to marriage as God has to his promises with his people. We need passion in the marriage relationship to keep the commitment and intimacy satisfying, but this passion should be focused exclusively on our spouse.

Deuteronomy 24:1-4 Some might view this regulation as proof that God supports divorce. On the contrary, God hates divorce (Malachi 2:16). Regulations like this were given to put controls on this unsatisfactory solution for disunity in marriage.

Deuteronomy 24:1-4 Some think this passage supports divorce, but that is not the case. It simply recognizes a practice that already existed in Israel. All four verses must be read to understand the point of this passage. It certainly is not suggesting that a man divorce his wife on a whim. Divorce was a permanent and final act for the couple. Once divorced and remarried to others, they could never be remarried to each other. This restriction was to prevent casual remarriage after a frivolous separation. The intention was to make people think twice before divorcing. (NIV)

Deuteronomy 24:1-4 Certain legitimate grounds for a divorce are permitted. Shameful or indecent acts = sexual immorality. (PDR)

Deuteronomy 24:1-4 The woman is not condemned for remarrying another man. (PDR)

Matthew 5:31 Jesus said that divorce is not permissible except for unfaithfulness. This does not mean that divorce should automatically occur when a spouse commits adultery. The word "unfaithfulness" implies a sexually immoral lifestyle, not a confessed and repented act of adultery. Those who discover that their partner has been unfaithful should first make every effort to forgive, reconcile, and restore their relationship. We are always to look for reasons to restore the marriage relationship rather than for excuses to leave it.

5:31-32 Divorce is as hurtful and destructive today as in Jesus' day. God intends marriage to be a lifetime commitment (Genesis2:24). When entering into marriage, people should never consider divorce an option for solving problems or a way out of a relationship that seems dead. In these verses, Jesus is attacking those who purposely abuse the marriage contract by using divorce to satisfy their lustful desire to marry someone else. Are your actions today helping your marriage grow strong, or are you tearing it apart?

Matthew 19:3-6 to: Jesus affirms the importance of the marriage relationship. We may find it confining to be without an "escape hatch" in marriage, but God has always intended that marriage be a lifelong relationship.

19:7-8 Moses' law, which is found in Deuteronomy 24:1-4 allowed a man to divorce his wife by writing a formal letter of dismissal. It also, it included that the man and woman could not later remarry. Jesus said that Moses gave this law only because of people's hard hearts. Because sinful human nature made divorce inevitable, Moses instituted some laws to help its victims. These were civil laws designed especially to protect the women who in that culture were quite vulnerable when living alone. Because of Moses' law, a man could no longer just throw his wife out, he had to write this letter and thus think twice about divorce. Instead of looking for reasons to leave each other, couples should concentrate on how to stay together. It is important to correct the attitudes, behaviors and root problems that bring on conflicts in marriage and learn to work through such situations.

Mark 10:11-12 Jesus continues to explain to his disciples other ways that men and women commit adultery. In our society, many believe divorce to be a good way to deal with conflict. Most of us have discovered, however, that intrapersonal conflict (problems we have within ourselves) follows us wherever we go. It is only an evidence of much deeper problems. Marriage is not always easy and neither is spiritual growth but, both can be of great help to each other.

Luke 16:18 Most religious leaders of Jesus' day permitted a man to divorce his wife for nearly any reason. Jesus' teaching about divorce went far beyond Moses (Deuteronomy 24:1-4). Stricter than any of the schools of thought. Jesus' teachings shocked his hearers (see Matthew 19:10) just as they shake today's readers. Jesus says in no uncertain terms that marriage is a lifetime commitment. To leave your spouse for another person may be legal, but it is adultery in God's eyes. As you think about marriage, remember that God intends it to be a permanent commitment. (NIV)

Luke 16:18 Marriage is sacred (PDR)

1 Corinthians 7:28 Many people think that marriage will solve all their problems. Here are some problems marriage won't solve (1) loneliness, (2) sexual temptation, (3) satisfaction of one's deepest emotional needs, (4) elimination of life's difficulties. Marriage alone does not hold two people together, commitment to Christ and to each other despite conflicts and problems does. As wonderful as it is, marriage does not automatically solve every problem. (NIV)

1 Corinthians 7:10-11 These verse exhorts us not to divorce, but if separated to <u>wait</u> patiently. (PDR)

1 Corinthians 7:12-14 Paul's command about the permanence of marriage comes from the Old Testament (Genesis 2:24) and from Jesus (Mark 10:2-10). His suggestion in this verse is based on God's command and Paul applies it to the situation the Corinthians were facing. Because of their desire to serve Christ, some people in the Corinthian church thought they ought to divorce their pagan spouses and marry Christians. But Paul affirms the marriage commitment. God's ideal is for marriages to stay together, even when one spouse is an unbeliever. The Christian spouse should try to win the other over to Christ. Paul makes a strong case for staying with the unbelieving spouse and being a positive influence on the marriage. Paul, like Jesus, believe that marriage is permanent. (see Mark 10:1-9)

1 Corinthians 7:15-16 This verse is misused by some as a loophole to get out of marriage. But Paul's statements are given to encourage the Christian spouse, to try to get along with the unbeliever and to make the marriage work. If however the unbelieving spouse insist on leaving, Paul says to let him or her go. The only alternative will be for the Christian to deny his or her faith to preserve the marriage. Paul's chief purpose in writing this is to urge the married couples to seek unity, not separation.

1 *Corinthians* 7:17 Paul says that people should be Christians where they are. You can do God's work and demonstrate your faith anywhere. If you became a Christian after marriage, and your spouse is not a believer, remember that you don't have to be married to a Christian to live for Christ. Don't assume that you are in the wrong place or stuck with the wrong person. You may be just where God wants you.

1 *Corinthians* 7:16-17 Encourages us to retain our marital relationship and wait for God to work. (PDR)

1 *Corinthians* 7:27-28 Commitment is important to those who marry, honor your vows by sticking with your spouse. (NLT).

1 *Corinthians* 7:28 Reveals that remarriage is not a sin. (PDR)

Self Reflection

1. How does this topic apply to me?

2. What truths in this area can I recognize and fully address?

3. What Bible verses here best encourage and inspire me to want to be a better husband in this area?

4. What steps can I begin to take today to safeguard my marriage from divorce, or if close to divorce how do I turn things around?

5. Who can I reach out to for personal help and support in this area? (This could be a family member, friend, professional counselor, a spiritual leader or someone you worship with)

Journal

11. God's Catalog of Sexual Sins

God makes it very clear in the Bible what sexual sins are and how to avoid them. Certain sexual sins seem more obvious than others and yet certain sexual sins are more socially accepted in today's time. My sexual sin was breaking the eighth commandment of the Ten Commandments...*Do not commit adultery*. We hear about this sin in the news everyday and it affects men from all walks of life. It brought a president of the United States to the verge of an impeachment trial, it forced a New York governor to resign early from his elected position and wrecked havoc and broke up the marriage of one of the worlds top sports figure, Tiger Woods. But even with this type of sin getting so much exposure in the media, we men continue to run the same game and think that we won't get caught. I thought that I could get away with it on a very conscious level, many times saying to God that I'm going to stop this behavior. I had to hit a brick wall before I was able to stop and rethink about what I was doing, how I was hurting God, my wife and family. While I engaged in this sin, it led to other sins. I began lying to my wife and family trying to cover up my activity. I stole time from them and gave it to someone else. I coveted someone who did not belong to me. I had to learn that my wife and family belonged to me, and I belonged to them and not anyone else.

The "Men's Code" says that it's cool and okay to do this stuff, as long as you don't get caught. This code goes deeper when it comes to sexual sin. It allows us to think that many kinds of sexual sin are okay and acceptable. This thinking and behavior is totally wrong and always results in many people being hurt spiritually, morally and physically. I believe most sexual sins are done out of ignorance, selfishness, or rebellion against God. God places a moral compass in all of us, some of us simply refuse to use it. I operated out of selfishness and rebellion, having had many opportunities to stop the behavior, but decided to continue being out of control. In God's eyes, all sin is equal and separates us from Him. If there is any sexual sin or sins that you are now involved with, know that after reading Exodus 20:14, Leviticus 18:6-23, Deuteronomy 22:5, Deuteronomy 23:17-18 and other biblical texts that it should be clear about what's right and wrong regarding all sexual behavior for a man and woman. Those who do so in ignorance after reading what the Bible has to say on this topic will no longer have an excuse for their behavior. Can you turn this around? The answer is yes! Will it be easy to do? No, but with faith, belief and trust in God, it is possible to break away from any sin. I was able to accomplish this by surrendering to God, accepting His help and with His earthly angels he provided.

What helped me the most through my struggle with sexual sin was getting the professional and spiritual counseling and remaining dedicated to the process. I also had to totally cut off seeing or speaking with the person I had the affair with. Then my next steps were to stop associating with people or places that could tempt me back to sin, stop viewing books, pictures or images that encourages bad sexual behavior and began focusing on God's Word in the Bible about how to become a virtuous man. Seek help before you hurt someone you love and ruin your life. It took getting exposed for me to humble myself before God and my wife before I was able to begin trying to turn things around. Moreover, I had to be willing to be open to hear, receive, study, and apply the Word of God to my life. I now know that God has forgiven me for my past sins, and He can forgive each and everyone of you who may now be lost and stuck in some sexual sin. You can start by confessing your sin to God and others, repent and turn away from it. The following verses serve as a constant reminder of what God's laws are for right sexual living.

Bible Study-Chapter 11

Exodus 20:14 The Ten Commandments state…Do not commit adultery (Commandment #8)

Exodus 20:17 The Ten Commandments state…Do not covet your neighbor's wife. (Commandment #10)

Leviticus 18:6-23 key *verses include* (6) You must never have sexual intercourse with a close relative, for I am the Lord. (7) Do not violate your father by having sexual intercourse with your mother. She is your mother; you must never have intercourse with her. (8) Do not have sexual intercourse with any of your father's wives, for this would violate your father. (9) Do not have sexual intercourse with your sister or halve sister, whether she is your father's daughter or your mother's daughter, whether she was brought up in the same family or somewhere else. (10) Do not have sexual intercourse with your granddaughter, with your son's daughter or your daughter's daughter; that would violate you. (11) Do not have sexual intercourse with the daughter of any of your father's wives; she is your half sister. (12) Do not have intercourse with your aunt, your father's sister, because she is your father's close relative. (13) Do not have sexual intercourse with your aunt, your mother's sister, because she is your mother's close relative. (14) And do not violate your uncle, your father's brother, by having sexual intercourse with his wife, she is also your aunt. (15) Do not have sexual intercourse with your daughter-in-law, she is your son's wife. 16) Do not have intercourse with your brother's wife, this would violate your brother. (17) Do not have sexual intercourse with both a woman and her daughter, or daughter's daughter. They are close relatives, and to do this would be a horrible wickedness. (18) Do not marry a woman and her sister because they will be rivals. But if your wife dies, then it is all right to marry her sister. (19) Do not violate a woman by having sexual intercourse with her during her menstrual impurity. (20) Do not defile yourself by having sexual intercourse with your neighbor's wife. (22) Do not practice homosexuality; it is a detestable sin. (23) A man must never defile himself by having sexual intercourse with an animal and a woman must never present herself to a male animal in order to have intercourse with it; this is a terrible perversion.

Deuteronomy 22:5 A woman must not wear men's clothing, and a man must not wear women's clothing. The Lord your God detests people who do this.

Deuteronomy 23:17-18 (17) No Israelite man or woman may ever become a temple prostitute. (18) Do not bring to the house of the Lord your God any offering from the earnings of a prostitute, whether a man or a woman, for both are detestable to the Lord your God.

Romans 1:24-29 key verses include (26) That is why God abandoned them to their shameful desires. Even the women turned against the natural way to have sex and instead indulged in sex with each other. (27) And the men, instead of having normal sexual relationships with women, burned with lust for each other. Men did shameful things with each other men and as a result, suffered within themselves the penalty they so richly deserved. (28) When they refused to acknowledge God, he abandoned them to their evil minds and let them do things that should never be done

Consequences of and Confronting Immorality In Our Community

1 *Corinthians* **5** *key verses include* (1) Paul speaking…"I can hardly believe the report about the sexual immorality going on among you. Something so evil that even the pagans don't do it. I am told that you have a man in your church who is living in sin with his father's wife. (2) And you are so proud of yourselves! Why aren't you mourning in sorrow and shame? And why haven't you removed this man from your fellowship? (3) Even though I am not there in person, I am with you in the spirit. Concerning the one who has done this, I have already passed judgment (4) in the name of the Lord Jesus. You are to call a meeting of the church, and I will be there in spirit, and the power of the Lord Jesus will be with you as you meet. (5) Then you must cast this man out of the church and into Satan's hands, so that his sinful nature will be destroyed and he himself will be saved when the Lord returns. (6) How terrible that you should boast about your spirituality, and yet you let this sort of thing go on. Don't you realize that if even one person is allowed to go on sinning, soon all will be affected? (7) Remove this wicked person from among you so that you can stay pure. (9) When I wrote to you before, I told you not to associate with people who indulge in sexual sin. (10) But I wasn't talking about unbelievers who indulge in sexual sin, or who are greedy or who are swindlers or idol worshipers. You would have to leave this world to avoid people like that. (11) What I meant was that you are not to associate with anyone who claims to be a Christian, yet indulges in sexual sin, or is greedy, or worships idols, or is abusive, or a drunkard, or a swindler. Don't even eat with such people. (12) It isn't my responsibility to judge outsiders, but it certainly is your job to judge those inside the church who are sinning in these ways. (13) God will judge those on the outside; but as Scriptures say, "You must remove the evil person from among you."

Study Application Notes

Exodus 20:17 To covet is to desire what another person has. We are not to set our desires on anything that belongs to someone else. Not only can such desires make us miserable, they can also lead us to other sins such as adultery, lying and stealing. This commandment insists that we guard our thoughts.

Leviticus 18:6-18 Marrying relatives was prohibited by God for physical, social, and moral reasons. Children born to near relatives may experience serious health problems. Without these specific laws, sexual promiscuity would have more likely occurred first in families.

18:6-23 Several abominations or wicked actions are listed here, (1) having sexual relations with close relatives, (2) committing adultery, (3) offering children as sacrifices, (4) having homosexual relations and (5) having sexual relations with animals. Such practices lead to disease, deformity and death; they disrupt family life and society and reveal a low regard for the value of one's self and others. Society today takes some of these practices lightly, even trying to make them acceptable. But they are still sins in God's eyes. If you consider them acceptable, you are not judging by God's standards.

Deuteronomy 22:5 This verse commands men and women not to reverse or confuse their sexual roles. The Bible is unequivocal on this point. Men, rejoice in your maleness. Women, rejoice in your femaleness. Today role rejections are common; there are some men who want to become women and some women who want to become men. Be the sexual gender God intended you to be, in your appearance, in your clothing, and in your thinking. God had a purpose in making us uniquely male and female.

Deuteronomy 23:17-18 Prostitution is not overlooked in God's law, it is strictly forbidden. However, during Moses' time, almost every religion known then included prostitution as an integral part of its worship. Prostitution makes a mockery out of God's original idea for sex, treating sex as a purely physical act rather than as an act of commitment to another. Outside of marriage, sex destroys relationships. Within marriage, approached with the right attitude, it can be a relationship builder. Sexual purity is often considered something to be embarrassed about. Healthy marriages must be founded upon trust, which is based on sexual purity. God frequently has to warn people against the practice of extramarital sex. Today we still need to hear his warning, young people need to be reminded about premarital sex, and adults need to be reminded about sexual infidelity.

Romans 1:26-27 God's plan for natural sexual relationships is his ideal for his creation. Unfortunately, sin distorts the natural use of God's gifts. Sin often means not only denying God, but also denying the way we are made. When people say that any sex act is acceptable as long as nobody gets hurt, they are fooling themselves. In the long run (and often in the short run), sin hurts people, individuals, spouses, families and whole societies.

1:26-27 Homosexuality (to exchange or abandon natural relations of sex) was as widespread in Paul's day as it is in ours. Many pagan practices encouraged it. God is willing to receive anyone who comes to him in faith, and Christians should love and accept others no matter what their background. Yet homosexuality is strictly forbidden in Scripture (Leviticus 18:22) Homosexuality is considered an acceptable practice by many in our world today, even by some Churches. But society does not set the standard for God's law. Many homosexuals believe that their desires are normal and that they have a right to express them. But God does not obligate or encourage us to fulfill all our desires (even seemingly normal ones). Those desires that violate his laws must be controlled. Remember, God can and will forgive sexual sins just as he forgives other sins.

1 Corinthians 5:1-5 We face many of the same forms of sexual immorality that the Corinthians faced. Like the people of Corinth, we tend to put on a blindfold and tell ourselves that everything is all right. The church must discipline flagrant sin among its members; such sins left unchecked can hurt and paralyze churches, communities and families. The correction however should never be vengeful. Instead, it should be given to help bring about a cure. Paul was telling the church that it had a responsibility to maintain the standards of morality found in God's commandments. God tells us not to judge others. But he also tells us not to tolerate flagrant sin because leaving that sin undisciplined will have a dangerous influence on other believers.

5:6-7 Paul calls for the Corinthians to remove the unrepented sinner from among their fellowship. If they don't do it, his or her destructive activities would eat away at their church fellowship like a cancer.

5:9-13 Paul makes it clear that we should not dissociate ourselves from unbelievers, otherwise we cannot carry out Christ's command to tell them about salvation (Matthew 28:18-20). But, we are to dissociate ourselves from the person who claims to be a Christian, yet indulges in and rationalizes sins explicitly forbidden in Scripture.By rationalizing sin, a person harms others for whom Christ died and dims the image of God in himself or herself.

Self Reflection

1. How does this topic apply to me?

2. What truths in this area can I recognize and how can I fully address them?

3. Which Bible verses here best encourage and inspire me to want to be a better husband, father and man in this area?

4. What steps can I begin to take today to strengthen myself in this area?

5. Who can I reach out to for personal help and support in this area? (This could be a family member, friend, professional counselor, a spiritual leader or someone you worship with)

Journal

12. Avoiding Sexual Sin, Lust and Excess

In order to avoid and not embrace sexual sin, one has to master not embracing sexual temptation. One leads to the other. The Apostle Paul in I Corinthians 6:18 states, *"Run away from sexual sin."* This means to quickly move away from any tempting situations you may encounter. We men must relearn this strategy when encountering this path. In the music industry and being a musician this presented a challenge to me, to remain pure among the glutton of girly temptations surrounding you. Some of us walk right into sexually tempting situations instead of avoiding them. Then when you're in the center of it you want to go deeper and the lust can become excessively stronger. One way the *"Men's Code"* encourages us to fantasize about sexual sin is by staring and lusting emphatically at females' sexual body parts. This can be most obvious to everyone except the man who indulges himself in the mental foreplay.

This habit is quickly passed on to young men and male children as they observe their dads, brothers, and friends do it. This type of foreplay can lead to men to desiring sexual fulfillment and the ultimate conquest of their arousal. If not right at that moment, he will most likely contemplate how he can achieve his sexual conquest at a later time. My times of embracing sexual sin usually left me feeling guilty, or that I could somehow rationalize it in some meaningless way. I became cold and callous to God's consequences for this behavior. Today I'm grateful that God has humbled me to seek His strength, correction, and guidance. God's Code is the main tool I now embrace to keep me strong in this area of avoidance. Proverbs 3:5 *says "Trust in the Lord with all your heart and lean not on your own understanding." Prov 23:26: My son, give me your heart and let your eye keep to my ways.* This meant that I would now start trusting and obeying God's Word and teachings in this area. I would recommit to honoring my marriage vows and stop hurting and dishonoring God, my wife, and family. Romans 12:2 says *"Do not conform any longer to the pattern of this world, but be transformed by the renewing of your mind. Then you will be able to test and approve what God's will is, His good pleasing and perfect will"* (NIV). God's will is never for us to go commit adultery on our spouses and to destroy our families.

Practically speaking, this renewing of our minds calls for a different way of controlling our thoughts and not reacting to sexual temptations. You no longer feed your thoughts with images, places or people who can trigger you being out of control. You no longer desire or seek outside stimuli to enhance your sexual satisfaction with your wife. You stop going to places and locations that you know will tempt you to consider doing the wrong thing. You replace lustful thoughts of the women you see and come in contact with, with thoughts of inner beauty, Godly love, and righteousness. You kick to the curb any old friends, acquaintances or habits that bring you into the land of the lost. I now cling to God, His Word, friends, and family who love the Lord and are there to hold me accountable for my actions.

I remain faithful to my Godly spouse being ever so satisfied with God's companion gift to me. I now embrace God's Code to direct my thinking and actions in this area. Proverbs 5:18-20 states: *Let your wife be a fountain of blessing for you. Rejoice in the wife of your youth. She is a loving doe, a graceful deer. (19) Let her breasts satisfy you always. May you always be captivated by her love.*

These Bible verses confirm to me that God wants us to be satisfied and content with the one spouse He has given you. We cannot buy into the Men's Code perception of Solomon and his many wives. That's the thinking that it's okay to have your wife and other women on the side. Use your moral and spiritual compass to keep you remaining in God's light. What follows are some of God's Codes to help us avoid sexual sin, lust and excess. These Bible verses confirm that God wants us to be satisfied and content with our spouse only. We cannot buy into the "Men's Code" perception of Solomon and his many wives. That's the thinking that prescribes that it's okay to have your wife and other women on the side. Use your spiritual and moral compass to keep you living in God's truths. What follows are some of "God's Codes" to help us avoid sexual sin, lust and excess.

Bible Study-Chapter 12

1 *Corinthians Chapter 6:9-20 Key verse include* (9) Don't you know that those who do wrong will have no share in the Kingdom Of God? Those who indulge in sexual sin, who are idol worshipers, adulterers, male prostitutes, homosexuals, (10) thieves, greedy people, drunkards, abusers and swindlers, none of these will have a share in the Kingdom of God. (11) There was a time when some of you were just like that, but now your sins have been washed away, and you have been set apart by God. You have been made right with God because of what the Lord Jesus Christ and the Spirit of our God have done for you. (12) You may say, "I am allowed to do anything" But I reply, "Not everything is good for you. And even though I am allowed to do anything, I must not become a slave to anything." (13)…But our bodies were not made for sexual immorality. They were made for the Lord, and the Lord cares about our bodies. (15) Should a man take his body, which belongs to Christ, and join it to a prostitute? Never! (16) And don't you know if a man joins himself to a prostitute, he becomes one body with her? For the Scriptures say, "The two are united into one." (17) But the person who is joined to the Lord becomes one spirit with him. (18) Run away from sexual sin! No other sin so clearly affects the body as this one does. For sexual immorality is a sin against your own body. (19) Or don't you know that your body is the temple of the Holy Spirit who lives in you and was given to you by God? You do not belong to yourself. (20) for God bought you with a high price. So you must honor God with your body.

Galatians 5:17-25 (17) The old sinful nature loves to do evil, which is just the opposite from what the Holy Spirit wants. And the Spirit gives us desires that are opposite from what the sinful nature desires. These two forces are constantly fighting each other, and your choices are never free from this conflict. (18) But when you are directed by the Holy Spirit, you are no longer subject to the law. (19) "When you follow the desires of your sinful nature, your lives will produce these evil results: sexual immorality, impure thoughts, eagerness for lustful pleasure (20) idolatry, participation in demonic activities, hostility, quarrelling, jealousy, outburst of anger, selfish ambition, divisions of the feeling that everyone is wrong except those in your own little group, (21) envy, drunkenness, wild parties, and other kinds of sin. Let me tell you again, as I have before, that anyone living that sort of life will not inherit the Kingdom of God. (22) But when the Holy Spirit controls our lives, he will produce this kind of fruit in us: love, joy, peace, patience, kindness, goodness, faithfulness, gentleness, and self-control. Here there is no conflict with the law. (24) Those who belong to Christ Jesus have nailed their passions and desires of their sinful nature to the cross and crucified them there. (25) If we are now living by the Holy Spirit, let us follow the Holy Spirit's leading in every part of our lives.

Ephesians 5:1-7 (1) Follow God's example in everything you do, because you are his children. (2) <u>Live a life filled with love for others,</u> following the example of Christ, who loved you and gave himself as a sacrifice to take away your sins. And God was pleased, because that sacrifice was like sweet perfume to him. (3) Let there be no sexual immorality, impurity or greed among you. Such sins have no place among God's people. (4) Obscene stories, foolish talk and coarse jokes, these are not for you. Instead, let there be thankfulness to God. (5) You can be sure that no immoral, impure, or greedy person will inherit the Kingdom of God. For a greedy person is really an idolater who worships the things of the world. (6) <u>Don't be fooled by those who try to excuse these sins,</u> for the terrible anger of God comes upon all who disobey him. (7) don't participate in the things these people do.

Proverbs 22:14 the mouth of immoral women is a deep pit; those living under the Lord's displeasure will fall in to it.

Proverbs 23:26-28 My son, give me your heart and let your eyes keep to my ways, (27) for a prostitute is a deep pit and a wayward wife is a narrow well. (28) Like a bandit she lies in wait and multiples the unfaithful among men. (NIV)

1 Kings 11:1-12 key verses include (1) Now Solomon loved many foreign woman. Besides Pharaoh's daughter, he married women from both Moab, Ammon, Edom, Sidon and from among the Hittites, (2) The Lord clearly had instructed his people not to intermarry with those nations, because the women they married would lead them to worship their gods. Yet Solomon insisted on loving them anyway. (3) He had seven hundred wives and three hundred concubines. And sure enough they led his heart away from the Lord. (4) In Solomon's old age, they turned his heart to worship their gods instead of trusting in the Lord his God, as his father, David had done. (6) Thus, Solomon did what was evil in the Lord's sight, he refused to follow the Lord completely, as his father David had done. (9) The Lord was very angry with Solomon, for his heart had turned away from the Lord, the God of Israel, who had appeared to him twice. (10) He had warned Solomon specifically about worshiping other gods, but Solomon did not listen to the Lord's command. (11) So now the Lord said to him, "Since you have not kept my covenant and have disobeyed my laws, I will surely tear the kingdom away from you and give it to one of your servants. (12) But for the sake

of your father, David, I will not do this while you are still alive. I will take the kingdom away from your son. (13) And even so, I will let him be king of one tribe, for the sake of my servant David and the sake of Jerusalem, my chosen city.

Study Application Notes

1 *Corinthians Chapter 6:9-11* Paul is describing characteristics of unbelievers. He doesn't mean that idolaters, adulterers, prostitutes, homosexuals, thieves, greedy people, drunkards, slanders, or swindlers are automatically and irrevocably excluded from heaven. Christians come out of all kinds of different backgrounds, including these. They may still struggle with evil desires, but they should not continue in these practices. Paul clearly states that even those who sin in these ways can have their lives changed by Christ. However those who say they are Christians but persist in these practices without any sign of remorse will not inherit the kingdom of God. Such people need to evaluate their lives to see if they truly believe in Christ.

6:9-11 In a permissive society, it is easy for people to overlook or tolerate some immoral behaviors (adultery, greed, drunkenness, etc) while remaining outraged at others (homosexuality, thievery). We must not participate in sin or condone it in any way, nor may we be selective about what we condemn or excuse. Staying away from more acceptable forms of sin is difficult, but God expects his followers to have high standards.

6:13 Sexual immorality is a temptation that is always before us, in movies and on television, sex outside marriage is treated as a normal, even desirable, part of life, while marriage is often shown as a confining and joyless. We can even be looked down on by others if we are suspected of being pure. But God does not forbid sexual sin just to be difficult. He knows its power to destroy us physically and spiritually. No one should under estimate the power of sexual immorality. It has devastated countless lives, and destroyed families, churches, communities and even nations. God wants to protect us from damaging ourselves and others, so he desires to fill us, our loneliness, our desires, with himself.

6:15-17 This teaching about sexual immorality and prostitutes was especially important for the Corinthian church because the temple of the love goddess Aphrodite was in Corinth. This temple employed more than a thousand prostitutes as priestess and sex was part of the worship ritual. Paul clearly states that Christians are to have no part in sexual immorality, even if it is acceptable and popular in our culture.

6:19-20 What did Paul mean when he said that our bodies belong to God? Many people say they have the right to do whatever they want with their own bodies. Although they think that this is freedom, they are really enslaved to their own desires. When we become Christians, the Holy Spirit fills and lives in us. Therefore, we no longer own our bodies. "Bought at a price" refers to slaves purchased at auction. Christ's death freed us from sin, but also obligates us to his service. Because your body belongs to God, you must not violate his standards for living.

Galatians 5:16-21 Very often, God's will for us stands in direct opposition to our natural desires. We must see this truth and be willing to turn away from following our own selfish desires and redirect our course back to doing God's will as revealed in the Bible. Here we find a whole list of destructive behaviors that flow out of a self-centered life. When we turn our lives over to God, however we allow his Spirit to help control the desires that lead us to sin. More and more God's desires become our own desires. Considering the facts, submitting our lives to God's will is the best choice we can make.

Galatians 5:17 Paul describes the two forces conflicting within us, the Holy Spirit and the sinful nature (our evil desires or inclinations which stem from our bodies) Paul is not saying that these forces are equal, the Holy Spirit is infinitely stronger. But if we rely on our own wisdom, we will make wrong choices. If we try to follow the Holy Spirit by our own human effort, we will fail. We all have evil desires, and we can't ignore them. In order to follow the Holy Spirit's guidance, we must deal with them decisively (crucify them). Our only way to freedom from our evil desires is through the empowering of the Holy Spirit.

Galatians 5:22-24 These characteristics are a product of the Holy Spirit's work in a life submitted to God and his plan. Just as a tree bears fruit by means of God's silent work behind the scenes, we produce this fruit of the Spirit by means of God's power alone. Our part is to surrender our lives to him. When the Holy Spirit begins to bear this fruit in us, sin loses its power. If we want the fruit of the Spirit to grow in us, we must join our lives to his. We must know him, love him, remember him and imitate him. With joy and peace we overcome the pain of our broken past. With love, kindness, goodness, faithfulness, and gentleness we restore our relationships and make restitution. With patience we persevere through the difficult times. With self-control we stand against temptation. God's Spirit can supply everything we need for fruitful lives.

Ephesians 5:1-5 God wants us to follow his will for our lives. Some of us may wonder how we can know what God wants us to do. Here we see that God wants us to be like Jesus Christ. As we look at his life, we can see how God would like us to think and act. We are to love our enemies, just as Jesus did. We are to avoid sexual impurity, greed and obscene speech since they stand counter to the character of God. How can we praise God and remind others of his goodness when we are speaking coarsely? As difficult as imitating Christ might sound, anything is possible with God's powerful help.

Ephesians 5:5-7 Paul is not forbidding all contacts with unbelievers, Jesus taught his followers to befriend sinners and lead them to him. Instead Paul is speaking against condoning the lifestyle of people who make excuses for bad behavior and recommend its practice to others.

1 Kings 11:3 For all his wisdom, Solomon had some weak spots. He could not say no to compromise or to lustful desires. Whether he married to strengthen political alliances or to gain personal pleasure, these foreign wives lead him into idolatry. You may have strong faith, but you also have weak spots, and that is where temptation usually strikes. Strengthen and protect your weaker areas because a chain is only as strong as its weakest link. If Solomon, the wisest man could fall, so can you.

1 Kings 11:4 In marriage and close friendships it is difficult to resist the pressure to compromise. Our love leads us to identify with the desires of those we care about. It is because we want to please our loved ones that God asked us not to marry those who do not share our commitment to him. This is also why God instructed Solomon not to marry women from foreign nations. He chose to disregard God's commands and married many foreign women who subsequently lead him away from God. God became very angry with Solomon and punished him for his disobedience.

1 Kings 11:9-10 Solomon didn't turn away from God all at once or in a brief moment. His spiritual coldness started with a minor departure from God's laws. Over the years, that little sin grew until it resulted in Solomon's downfall. A little sin can be the first step in turning away from God. It is not the sins we don't know about, but the sins we excuse, that cause us the greatest trouble. We must never let any sin go unchallenged. In your life is an unchallenged sin spreading like a deadly cancer? Don't excuse it. Confess it to God and ask him for strength to resist temptation.

1 *Kings 11:11-13* Solomon's powerful and glorious kingdom could have been blessed for all time, instead it was approaching its end. Solomon had God's promises, guidance and answers to prayer, yet he allowed sin to remain all around him. Eventually it corrupted him so much that he was no longer interested in God. Solomon had begun by laying the foundation with God, but he did not follow thru in his latter years. As a result, he lost everything. It is not enough to get off to a right start in building our marriage on God's principles; we must remain faithful to God to the end. God must be in control of our lives from start to finish.

Self Reflection

1. How does this topic apply to me?

2. What truths in this area directly can I recognize and how can I fully address them?

3. What Bible verses here best encourage and inspire me to want to be a better husband, father and a better man in this area??

4. What steps can I begin to take today to strengthen myself in this area?

5. Who can I reach out to for personal help and support in this area? (This could be a family member, friend, professional counselor, a spiritual leader or someone you worship with)

Journal

Journal

13. Avoiding Temptation

2 Timothy 2:22 tell us to *"Run from anything that stimulates youthful lust."* But for many of us, we choose to do the opposite, running into anything that radiates lust. We see that object or person with lust in our heart and begin to lose our mind and run head on into it. At that point we are in the heat of the moment and can be tempted to spin out of control right into a wrong situation. This verse continues to read: *"Follow anything that makes you want to do right."* I interpret this as meaning to read the Bible and obey its teaching along with being around people who will hold you accountable, to help you to avoid any potential sinful situation. 1 Corinthians 10:13 reads: *"But remember that the temptations that come into your life are no different from what others experience. And God is Faithful. He will keep the temptation from becoming so strong that you can't stand up against it. When you are tempted, he will show you a way out so that you will not give in to it."* This reminds us that others have resisted temptations and so can we with God's help. This is great news for those who are currently struggling with temptations and are losing their battles."

The answer for me was to immediately begin trusting and obeying God's will, not mine. I had to realize that it was going to be God's power that would give me victory over this and I could do nothing on my own ability. But first, I needed to surrender to his love, mercy, and divine guidance. To put this firmly into my mind required practice and a new way of thinking as well. It's important to remember that temptation begins in our mind and with our thoughts. The *"Men's Code"* tells us that if it feels good then do it and think about the consequences latter. This code teaches men that it's okay to be selfish, self indulgent and foolish with our behaviors, particularly sexual temptation. It instructs men to embrace temptation at every corner and find ways to feed that temptation. For me avoiding temptation came down to connecting and embracing "God's Code', His written word and the desire to begin fully loving and respecting my wife as God calls us to do. I had to prepare my thinking in advance for any potential situation that temptation might present itself. This can be very subtle and requires thought and practice to undo acquired habits. I had to stop rationalizing and blaming others for my wrong behavior and accept responsibility for my actions. I began to tell our marriage counselor during our therapy sessions that I've got to change how I think about women, my wife and stop seeing and relating to them from a physical perspective. I needed to understand that God gave me my wife as a part to fulfill all of my desires and to complete me in every way. This I had to work on and it required time and patience on both my part and my wife's. But over time, "God's Code" began to triumph. Through much prayer, God's love and power, I was able to change, renew my thinking and my heart. Jesus was my model and inspiration. I decided that just as He resisted and was victorious over Satan's temptations for forty days (Matt 4:1-11) so would I. Another change I made was to begin being around people who would make me accountable for my actions and activities. I stopped engaging people whose thoughts were always of the flesh. I consciously sought to connect with men who took God's word seriously and were good examples of trying to live Godly lives. Today, I continue to involve myself with men who can help me to keep the right thoughts about staying in line with God's will. Even with this progress and renewal of heart, mind and soul, God will always test you. I have to remain on guard at all times against any form of temptation that could take me away from His path. Reading and studying scripture on this topic helps give me the tools to live a blameless life.

Bible Study-Chapter 13

Matthew 4:1-11 (1) Then Jesus was lead out into the wilderness by the Holy Spirit to be tempted there by the Devil. (2) For forty days and nights he ate nothing and became very hungry. (3) Then the Devil came and said to him, "If you are the Son of God, change these stones into loaves of bread" (4) But Jesus told him " No! The Scriptures say, 'People need more than bread for their life; they must feed on every word of God'. (5) Then the Devil took him to Jerusalem, to the highest point of the Temple, (6) and said " If you are the Son of God, jump off! For the Scriptures say, " He orders his angels to protect you. And they will hold you with their hands to keep you from striking your foot on a stone." (7) Jesus responded, " The Scriptures also say, Do not test the Lord your God." (8) Next the Devil took him to the peak of a very high mountain and showed him the nations of the world and all their glory. (9) "I will give it all to you" He said " if you will only kneel down and worship Me." (10) "Get out of here Satan," Jesus told him. For the Scriptures say, "You must worship the Lord your God; serve only Him. (11) then the Devil went away, and angels came and cared for Jesus.

1 *Corinthians 10:12-13* (12) If you think you are standing strong, be careful, for you too, may fall into the same sin. (13) But remember that the temptations that come into your life are no different from what others experience. And God is faithful. He will keep the temptation from becoming so strong that you can't stand up against it. When you are tempted, he will show you a way out so that you will not give in to it.

2 *Timothy 2:22* Run from anything that simulates youthful lust. Follow anything that makes you want to do right. Pursue faith, love and peace, and enjoy the companionship of those who call on the Lord with pure hearts.

Proverbs 5:8-9 (8) Run from her! Don't go near the door of her house. (9) If you do, you will lose your honor and hand over to merciless people everything you have achieved in life.

James 1:12-15 (12) God blesses the people who patiently endure testing. Afterward they will receive the crown of life that God has promised to those who love him. (13) And remember, no one who wants to do wrong should ever say, "God is tempting me." God is never tempted to do wrong, and he never tempts anyone else either. (14) Temptation comes from the lure of our own evil desires. (15) These evil desires leads to evil actions, and evil actions lead to death.

Psalms 19:12-13 (12) How can I know all the sins lurking in my heart? Cleanse me from these hidden faults. (13) Keep me from deliberate sins! Don't let them control me. Then I will be free of guilt and innocent of great sin.

Ephesians 6:11,13-18 (11) Put on all of God's armor so that you will be able to stand firm against all strategies and tricks of the Devil. (13) Use every piece of God's armor to resist the enemy in the time of evil, so that after the battle you will still be standing firm. (14) Stand your ground putting on the sturdy belt of truth and the body armor of God's righteousness. (15) For shoes, put on the peace that comes from the Good News, so that you will be fully prepared. (16) In every battle, you will need faith as your shield to stop the fiery arrows aimed at you by Satan. (17) Put on salvation as your helmet, and take the sword of the Spirit, which is the word of God. (18) Pray at all times and on every occasion in the power of the Holy Spirit. Stay alert and be persistent in your prayers for all Christians everywhere.

Study Application Notes

Matthew 4:1-11 This time of testing showed that Jesus was the Son of God, able to overcome the devil and his temptations. A person has not shown true obedience if he or she has never had an opportunity to be tested and to make the decision to obey or disobey. God wants to see whether or not we will really obey him. We will all be tested. Because we know that testing will come, we should be alert and ready for it. Remember your convictions are only strong if they hold up under pressure. The devil, also called Satan is real, not symbolic, and is constantly fighting against those who follow and obey God. Satan's temptations are real and he is always trying to get us to live his way or our way rather than God's way. If Jesus had given in, his mission on earth - to die for our sins and give us the opportunity to have eternal life would have been lost. When temptations seem especially strong, or when you think you can rationalize giving in, consider whether Satan may be trying to block God's purposes for your life or for someone else's life. This temptation by the devil gives us an example to follow when we are tempted. He would face temptation and not give in.

Matthew 4:3-4 Jesus was able to resist all of the devils temptations because he not only knew Scripture, but he also obeyed it. Knowing Bible verses is an important step in helping us resist Satan's attacks but we must obey the Word, not just know it.

1 *Corinthians 10:12-13* Paul gives strong encouragement about temptation. He says (1) wrong desires and temptations happen to everyone, so don't feel you've been singled out; (2) others have resisted temptation and so can you; (3) any temptations can be resisted because God will help you resist it. God helps you to resist temptation by helping you (1) recognize those people and situations that give you trouble, (2) run from anything you know is wrong, (3) choose to do only what is right, (4) pray for God's help, and (5) seek friends who love God and can offer help when you are tempted. Running from a tempting situation is your first step on the way to victory.

2 *Timothy 2:22* Paul's advice to Timothy is appropriate for us too. We need to run from the places and situations that are likely to lead to temptation. We are to avoid spending time with people who will lead us to a fall. Instead, we are to spend time with people who will support our spiritual growth. Do you have any recurring temptation that is difficult to resist? Remove yourself from any person or situation that stimulates your desire to sin.

James 1:12 The crown of life is like a victory wreath given to the winning athletes. God's crown of life is not glory and honor here on earth, but the reward of eternal life. The way to be in God's winner's circle is by loving him and staying faithful even under pressure.

James 1:13-14 People who live for God often wonder why they still have temptations. God test people, but he does not tempt them by trying to seduce them into sin. God does allow Satan to tempt people but, only to refine their faith and to help them grow in their dependence on Christ. We can resist the temptation to sin by turning to God for strength and choosing to obey his word.

James 1:13-15 Temptation comes from evil desires inside us, not from God. It begins with an evil thought and becomes sin when we dwell on the thought and allow it to become an action. Like a snowball rolling downhill, sin grows more destructive the more we let it have its way. The best time to stop a temptation is before it becomes too strong or moves too fast to control.

James 1:13-15 It is easy to blame others and make excuses for evil thoughts and wrong actions. Excuses include (1) it's the other person's fault; (2) I couldn't help it; (3) everybody's doing it; (4) It was just a mistake; (5) nobody's perfect; (6) the devil made me do it; (7) I was pressured in to it; (8) I didn't know it was wrong; (9) God is tempting me. A person who makes excuses is trying to shift the blame from himself or herself to something or someone else. A Godly person, on the other hand, accepts responsibility for his or her wrongs, confesses them and asks God for forgiveness.

Psalms 19:12-13 David asked God to reveal any hidden sins in his life so that he might see the truth. He was aware of his need to honestly examine his heart, and he asked God to help him. We have a tendency to be blind to our sins. We need God to clarify our thinking, to reveal the sin that is working its deception within us and to keep us from deliberately doing wrong. When our hearts are right with God, our actions will be right also.

Ephesians 6:11-13 While we may be firmly grounded in sound doctrine and accept our responsibility to live Godly lives, we need to be aware of the fierce, invisible warfare being waged against us. Our struggles could be the result of a direct attack by a spiritual enemy (anyone doing Satan's work or Satan himself, who is a vicious fighter). As we surrender our lives to God, he will stand with us in the battle. When we understand that our battle is not of this world, we will realize our need to depend on God's power instead of our own. _

Ephesians 6:13-18 Notice that each piece of our spiritual armor (except the sword) is defensive in nature. We need to make sure that each piece of the armor of God is operative in our lives. Truth, righteousness, faith and prayer will protect us against the assault of hostile spiritual forces. The forces arrayed against us are powerful, but the weapons God gives us are adequate for our defense Notice that a part of our armor, the shoes, enables us to share the Good News as we move forward in our spiritual lives.

Self Reflection

1. How does this topic apply to me?

2. What truths in this area can I recognize and how can I fully address them?

3. What Bible verses here best encourage and inspire me to want to be a better husband, father and a better man in this area?

4. What steps can I begin to take today to strengthen myself in this area?

5. Who can I reach out to for personal help and support in this area? (This could be a family member, friend, professional counselor, a spiritual leader or someone you worship with)

Journal

Journal

14. Exercising Self Control

To be sure, exercising self-control in the area of sexual purity for today's man is a huge challenge. This can be a very tough area for men to deal with and master. Modern society, the Internet, and scantily dressed women make it hard for most men to keep faithful in their marriage relations. Right? No, these are rationalizations that many men use to excuse our sinful behavior. Even when we know it's wrong, we lose our minds and can become unfaithful. After struggling with this issue for some time, I had to finally surrender to the Lord for his guidance, forgiveness and renewal of my mind. It took a whole new way of thinking about women and my wife most importantly to form a healthier attitude and mindset. It all begins in our minds: the evil desires and lusts we hold on to. Anytime we are looking sexually at a woman other than our wife and lusting after their body parts, we are at the beginning of what can lead to out of control sexual behavior. This for me included looking at pornography in magazines, x-rated movies, and x-rated internet sites. For many, this can lead a man to want to have real sex with a real woman and if you're not directing this towards your wife, you could be headed for deep trouble! This type of behavior is a form of adultery. In *Matthew 5:28*, Jesus said *"But I tell you that anyone who looks at a woman lustfully has already committed adultery with her in his heart."*

The "Men's Code" says to you, "It's okay to go have sex with that woman who's not your wife." The code encourages men not only to lose their minds, but also to lose their faith, honor, and respect with God and their wife. The "Men's Code" quickly aids our minds in creating lies and schemes to go after illicit sex and ways to cover up such behavior and activity. Following this path lead me to lose my self-control, putting me in situations that hurt my wife, family and most of all God! It took much study of God's written Word in the Bible for me to understand that God created sex for procreation and as an expression of love between a man and a wife. The good news is that "God's Code" offers us the solution of self-control. The story of Joseph and Potiphar's wife (Genesis 39:1-23) tells of how he resisted sexual advances and demands from her. It is a great example of how we should react to any sexual temptation we encounter. Run from it, or it becomes too easy to rationalize why we should engage in wrong behavior. After reconnecting to Christ through being baptized, I'm now better equipped to exercise self-control by turning to God in prayer and through daily reading of His Word in this area.

I read a book recommended by someone at my church's men's group that was very resourceful in this area. "Everyman's Battle" © (WaterBrook Press) offers some specific steps to take in our thinking about sexual purity. The book warns us that, *"Likewise we can be naïve and foolish regarding God's standard for sexual purity as we blindly stumble into wrong because everyone else is doing it."* It gives a very personal in-depth look into male sexual behavior and what tools and steps we can take to overcome this pitfall. This book gives the following definition on the goal of sexual purity: *"You are sexually pure when no sexual gratification comes from anyone or anything but your wife."* It tells us in the war of lust to build three defense perimeters into our life: (1) with your eyes (2) in your mind (3) in your heart. It is a must read for anyone struggling with sexual self control issues. Here are few of the book's recommended Scriptures regarding God's standard of sexual purity: Matthew 5:28, Romans 13:12-13, Mark 7:21-23, 1 Corinthians 6:18, Hebrews 13:4 and 1 Thessalonians 4:3-5,7.

I now frequently review the consequences of sexual infidelity to help me have a clear perspective on the importance of living righteously. In the back of this book in the reference section is a piece written by Randy Alcorn titled "Deterring Immorality by Counting It's Cost" The exorbitant price of sexual sin. This writing lists of all the specific consequences he could think of that would result from his immorality as a pastor and is useful to all of us to make a similar list. Sexual sin will always hurt your relationship with God, wife, family, friends, reputation and career. I am so blessed to be a witness that God saved my marriage, family, friendships, reputation and career from being ruined. I believe that my total willingness to admit to my mistakes, to take responsibility for them, to humble myself, to seek God and others help, to stick with it and to begin and continue to live a changed life is why God has granted His grace upon me. "God's Code" for living always wins out over the "Men's Code." We as men have to learn to surrender, accept and stop rejecting it. The good news is that God gives us the tools of scripture, faith, and His Holy Spirit to help us gain victory in this area. Having Godly minded friends and associates who hold me accountable for my actions, attending a good Bible teaching church and applying God's written Word daily is what has helped keep self control on the front burner in my life."

Bible Study-Chapter14

Genesis 39:1-23 (1) Now, when Joseph arrived in Egypt with the Ishmaelite traders, he was purchased by Potiphar, a member of the personal staff of Pharaoh. (2) The Lord was with Joseph and blessed him greatly as he served in the home of his Egyptian master. (3) Potiphar noticed this and realized that the Lord was with Joseph, giving him success in everything he did. (4) So Joseph naturally became quite a favorite of him. Potiphar soon put Joseph in charge of his entire household and entrusted him with all his business dealings. (5) From the day Joseph was put in charge, the Lord began to bless Potiphar for Joseph's sake. All his household affairs begin to run smoothly, and his crops and livestock flourished. (6) So Potiphar gave Joseph complete administrative responsibility over everything he own. With Joseph there, he didn't have a worry in the world, except to decide what he wanted to eat! Now Joseph was a very handsome and well-built young man. (7) And about this time, Potiphar's wife began to desire him (Joseph) and invited him to sleep with her. (8) But Joseph refused "Look", he told her, "My master trust me with everything in his entire household. (9) No one here has more authority than I do! He has held back nothing from me except you, because you are his wife. How could I ever do such a wicked thing? It would be a great sin against God" (10) She kept putting pressure on him day after day, but he refused to sleep with her, and he kept out of her way as much as possible. (11) One day, however no one else was around when he was doing his work around the house. (12) She came and grabbed him by his shirt, demanding, "Sleep with me!" Joseph tore himself away, but as he did, his shirt came off. She was left holding it as he ran from the house. (13) When she saw that she had his shirt and that he had fled, (14) she began screaming. Soon all the men around the place came running. "My husband has brought this Hebrew slave here to insult us!" she sobbed. "He tried to rape me, but I screamed. (15) When he heard my loud cries, he ran and left his shirt behind with me." (16) She kept the shirt with her, and when her husband came home that night, (17) "That Hebrew slave you've had around here tried to make a fool out of me," she said. (18) I was saved only by my screams. He ran out, leaving his shirt behind!" (19) After hearing his wife's story, Potiphar was furious! (20) He took Joseph and throw him in prison where the Kings prisoners were held. (21) But the Lord was with Joseph there too, and granted Joseph favor with the chief jailer. (22) Before long, the jailer put Joseph in charge of all the other prisoners and over everything that happened in the prison. (23) The chief jailer had no more worries after that, because Joseph took care of everything. The Lord was with him, making everything run smoothly and successfully.

Matthew 5:27-28 (27) "You have heard that the law of Moses says, "Do not commit adultery." (28) "But I say, anyone who even looks at a woman with lust in his eye has already committed adultery in his heart."

Mark 7:21-23 For within, out of a persons heart, come evil thoughts, sexual immorality, theft, murder, (22) adultery, greed, wickedness, deceit, eagerness for lustful pleasures, envy, slander, pride and foolishness. (23) All this vile things come from with in, they are what defile you and make you unacceptable to God.

1 Corinthians 6:18 Run away from sexual sin! No other sin so clearly affects the body as this one does. For sexual immorality is a sin against your own body.

Hebrews 13:4 Give honor to marriage and remain faithful to one another in marriage. God will surely judge people who are immoral and those who commit adultery.

1 Thessalonians 4:3-5,7 (3) God wants you to be holy, so you should keep clear of all sexual sin. (4) then each of you will control your body and live in holiness and honor (5) not in lustful passion as the pagans do, in their ignorance of God and his ways. (7) God has called us to be Holy, not to live impure lives.

Romans 6:12-14 (12) Do not let sin control the way you live, do not give in to its lustful desires. (13) Do not let any part of your body become a tool of wickedness, to be used for sinning. Instead give yourself completely to God since you have been given new life. And use your whole body as a tool to do what is right for the glory of God. (14) Sin is no longer your master, for you are no longer subject to the law, which enslaves you to sin. Instead, you are free by God's grace.

Romans 13:12-14 Clothe yourself with the amor of right living, as those who live in the light (13) We should be decent and true in everything we do, so that everyone can approve of our behavior. Don't participate in wild parties and getting drunk, or in adultery and immoral living, or in fighting and jealousy. (14) But let the Lord Jesus Christ take control of you, and don't think of ways to indulge your evil desires.

Study Application Notes

Genesis 39:2 God blessed Joseph even in the worst of circumstances. Even as a slave in a strange household in a foreign land, God made Joseph a success. We should not infer that God will also make us a success. We should not infer that God will also make us a successful. Rather, our chief goal should be to follow Joseph's example of being faithful to God's plan, no matter what the consequences.

7-12 Potiphar's wife failed to seduce Joseph, who resisted this temptation by saying it would be a sin against God. Joseph didn't say, "I'd be hurting you," or "I'd be sinning against Potiphar", or "I'd be sinning against myself." Such misdirected excuses easily cave in under pressure. ."Remember that sexual sin is not just between two consenting adults. It is an act of disobedience against God. Also Joseph avoided Potiphar's wife as much as possible. He refused her advances and finally ran from her. Sometimes merely trying to avoid the temptation is not enough. We must turn and run, especially when the temptations seem very strong as often is the case in sexual temptation.

19-20 Good guys often appear to finish last, the innocent seem to suffer. Here it looks as if Josephs' faithfulness to God was rewarded with years in prison. This may have discouraged Joseph, but it didn't stop him. Even in prison he continued living according to God's plan. In the end, after a number of setbacks, he was rewarded. We may need to look past present difficult circumstances to see that God has a purpose in our suffering. It may be an important part of our preparation for future work God has for us.

Matthew 5:27-28 The Old Testament law tells that it is wrong for a person to have sex with someone other than his or her spouse (*Exodus 20:14*). But Jesus tells that the desire to have sex with someone other than your spouse is mental adultery and thus sin. Jesus emphasizes that if the act is wrong, then so is the intention. To be faithful to your spouse with your body but not your mind is to break the trust so vital to a strong marriage. Jesus is not condemning natural interest in the opposite sex or even healthy sexual desire. Even the filling of one's mind with fantasies is considered evil in a sense, it is still sin!

Mark 7:21-23 Jesus explains that defilement does not start with our external behavior but comes from within our hearts. Most of us have tried to control our sinful natures by changing various aspects of our external behavior. The fact that this never works for long is clear evidence that our real problem lies within. We should find it encouraging that God goes right to the root of the problem: he works his healing from the inside out. By recognizing our need for internal healing, we open our lives to God's healing power.

1 *Corinthians 6:18* Sexual sin affects us like no other sin. It isn't that it is the heaviest on some imaginary sin scale, but rather, that its effects are broad and devastating. In sexual sin, we sin not only against ourselves but also against other people and God. Our bodies are the dwelling place of God's Holy Spirit, and they belong to God. This is one more reason for taking care of our bodies and seeking new life in Christ.

1 *Thessalonians 4:3-5* The Bible paints a clear picture of what God wants us to be like. Here Paul gives us a list of God's instructions regarding sexual sin. The temptation to engage in sexual intercourse outside the marriage relationship has always been powerful. Giving in to that temptation can have disastrous results. Sexual sins always hurt someone, individuals, families, businesses and churches. Beside the physical consequences there are also spiritual consequences. Sexual desires and activities must be placed under Christ's control. God created sex for procreation and pleasure, and as an expression of love between a husband and wife. Sexual experience must be limited to the marriage relationship to avoid hurting others, our relationship with God and ourselves.

Romans 6:12-14 Paul recognized that temptation would be an ongoing reality, so he gave us this warning: "Do not give in." The temptations we experience are extensions of the sinful natures that exist in each of us. Though we cannot overcome our sinful natures alone, we can ask God to help us. We are to reckon our sinful natures as crucified with Christ. As we call on the Lord, we have access to the Holy Spirit, who will help us overcome the powerful temptations in our lives.

Romans 13:12-13 People who live in the light are awake, their eyes open. They are not in the darkness of spiritual blindness, they have the ability to see and admit the truth about themselves. They strive to live a Godly life of right living in all that they do. Paul here lists some basic tenants for living such a life.

Romans 13:14 How do we let the Lord take control of us? First we identify with Christ by being baptized (Galatians 3:27: And all who have been united with Christ in baptism have been made like him), Second we exemplify the qualities Jesus showed while he was here on earth (love, humility, truth and service). We also must not give our desires any opportunity to lead us into sin. Avoid those situations that open the door to gratifying sinful desires.

Self Reflection

1. How does this topic apply to me?

2. What truths in this area do I recognize and how can I fully address them?

3. What Bible verses here best encourage and inspire me to want to be a better husband, father and man in this area?

4. What steps can I begin to take today to strengthen myself in this area?

5. Who can I reach out to for personal help and support in this area? (This could be a family member, friend, professional counselor, a spiritual leader or someone you worship with)

Journal

15. Deception, Dishonesty and Truth

Once you're deep into sin, doing something you know for sure is wrong and to continue that behavior, you want to hide it more and more. In fact you usually find yourself slipping deeper into that sin much like a snowball rolling down a hill. One can go through great lengths to deceive others with deception and dishonesty. Luke 12:2 states *"The time is coming when everything will be revealed, all that is secret will be made public."* I tried to hide the affair I was having on my wife. I would deceive her by saying I was going somewhere else when in fact I was going to get together with the other woman. I continued to keep up my deception and lies for several months before my wife began to pick up on what I was doing. Sure enough, she later confronted me with what I was doing. The time had come for everything I was doing in secret to be revealed. When faced with the truth, I continued to be in denial. I desperately tried to cling on to the *"Men's Code."* It kept telling me to lie myself out of this situation. But it wasn't working. The "Men's Code' had run its course... *"*

Although I had achieved much worldly success, God's will was also tugging at my heart and I was ready now to let him in. Remember that this code encourages men to keep cheating on their wives. It feeds us that it's okay not to be faithful and to break our marriage vows and to simply cover it up with deception and dishonesty. Here's the point when men have to decide whether to reject that thinking or to continue with the code which will eventually destroy your marriage. Thanks to the words of counsel and wisdom from my friend James, I was determined to break the Men's Code. The breaking came from wanting to embrace "God's Code" and this is what helped me get back on track. "God's Code", the inspired written Words of God provided the strength, power and courage to inspire me to change my behavior.

A combination of daily Bible study, weekly attending a Bible teaching church, having a God loving and forgiving wife and Godly minded friends helped to create in me a change, a heart of gratitude I came to learn that the truth will set you free even when it has hurt others. It will also set those whom you have hurt free and bring hope for the opportunity for healing and correction to take place Through much counseling my wife and I were able to get to the truth and begin to heal and repair our marriage. Being honest lead me to repent my sins and want to live a changed life. Leviticus 19:11 says *"Do not steal, do not cheat one another, do not lie."* When you have an affair on your spouse you commit these sins and more. I stole precious time, trust, and love from my wife and family. I cheated not only on my wife and family but also on myself and others who may have look up to me. Most of all I cheated on God who gave me the gift of love through my beautiful and loving wife. I lied to my wife, family, and friends, to myself. But most of all, I lied to God. The good news is that God forgives those who come to Him, ask for forgiveness, repent their sins and begin to live changed lives.

Bible Study-Chapter 15

Luke 12:2-3 (2) The time is coming when everything will be revealed; all that is secret will be made public. (3) Whatever you have said in the dark will be heard in the light, and whatever you have whispered in behind closed doors will be shouted from the housetops for all to hear!

Proverbs 10:9 The man of integrity walks securely, but he who takes crooked paths will be found out.

Proverbs 11:29 Those who brings trouble on their families inherit only wind. The fool will be a servant to the wise.

Proverbs 12:20 Deceit fills hearts that are plotting evil, joy fills hearts that are planning peace.

Proverbs 23:23 Get the truth and never sell it; also get wisdom, discipline, and good judgement.

Psalms 101:7 I will not allow deceivers to serve me, and liars will not be allowed to enter my presence

Leviticus 19:11 Do not steal, Do not cheat one another, Do not lie.

1 *Thessalonians 4:6* Never cheat a Christian brother in this matter by taking his wife, for the Lord avenges all such sins, as we have solemnly warned you before.

Exodus 20:15 Do not steal (one of the Ten Commandments #8)

20: 17 Do not covet your neighbor's house. Do not covet your neighbor's wife, male or female servant, ox or donkey or anything else your neighbor has. (One of the Ten Commandments #10)

Study Application Notes

Leviticus 19:11 God's plan for spiritual renewal demands honesty in both word and deed. Dishonesty and misrepresentation lead to suspicion, mistrust and hatred and ultimately destroying our relationships. Human relationships can only grow and thrive if we are willing to tell the truth, the only real basis for trust between people.

Exodus 20:15,17 Two of the Ten Commandments that deal with principles that define boundaries for healthy human relationships. Jesus summed up these human relational boundaries like this "Love your neighbor as yourself" (Matthew 22:39). This commandment assumes that we have cultivated a healthy self-respect and follow it up with loving actions that respect the boundaries of others.

Proverbs 11:29 One of the greatest recourses God gives us is the family. Families provide acceptance, encouragement, guidance and counsel. Bringing trouble of any kind on your family is foolish and harmful, because you cut yourself off from all that they provide. In your family strive for healing, communication and understanding.

Self Reflection

1. How does this topic apply to me?

2. What truths in this area can I recognize and how can I fully address them?

3. What Bible verses here best encourage and inspire me to want to be a better husband, father and a better man in this area?

4. What steps can I begin to take today to strengthen myself in this area?

5. Who can I reach out to for personal help and support in this area? (This could be a family member, friend, professional counselor, a spiritual leader or someone you worship with)

Journal

16. God's Advice and Consequences of Adultery

Faithfulness and purity in marriage is the one area that many men repeatedly fail to achieve. From David's story in the Bible (2 Samuel, Chapter 11-12) up to the present times we now live in, adultery is a huge problem in the world. It is the one area that if you break this commandment "Do not commit adultery" (Exodus 20:14), many of the other Ten Commandments will be broken as well. For example, to commit the act, one has to lie and bear false testimony to many including the one your engaging the act with, your wife, family and friends. To your wife or spouse you have perhaps killed their ability to love and trust you. It is as if you threw a dagger deep into their heart (thus breaking the "Thou shall not kill commandment"). Those who engage in this behavior become a thief who steals time, trust, and treasures from his wife and family. In having an affair one has to be absent from home on some basis, stealing time meant for family and giving it to someone else (thus breaking the "Thou shall not steal commandment"). We greatly hurt our spouses, family and God in engaging in adultery and the consequence become far-reaching and long lasting.

Most people who commit adultery go to great and calculated lengths to try and cover up their activities. In David's case (in the Bible) he went as far as to kill Uriah (Bathsheba's husband) and God's consequences were severe and had long-range effects. For me I tried to cover up my affair by keeping it far away in another city. I went to great lengths to try to deceive my wife into thinking that my absences where work related. I broke sacred areas of trust that have since took many years to rebuild. The "Men's Code" says that you should keep the affair going as long as it feels good and you don't get caught. The "Men's Code" says it's okay to be self-centered, full of pride and not care that you're greatly hurting your wife, family and God's Holy Covenant of marriage. This way of thinking directs men to buy into finding ways of rationalizing why to start and continue an affair. The consequences are devastating resulting in many men losing their minds, to disrespect and dishonor their marriage, and for many to lose their wives and families. God had to shut me down to get my attention. I had to remove pride and humble myself to clearly see the damage I caused my wife and family.

The good news is that "God's Code" was the one and only tool that was able to turn me away from sinful behaviors. Even more miraculous, God's healing power was able to repair, and restore our marriage. Although I was deeply lost in sin, I knew I loved my wife very much and wanted to stop hurting her and destroying our marriage. I desperately needed spiritual help and the practical guidance to make necessary changes in my life. When I searched for an alibi in hopes of deceiving my wife that I had not cheated, *God's Code* sent me a messenger friend, James (similar to Nathan in David's story). He told me that he could not cover and lie for me because he had once been in a similar situation. He and his wife were unable to work out their marriage and thus divorced. He told me that if I loved my wife and family, I should fight for them and do everything I could to turn things around. Most importantly he directed me to read God's Word on adultery (as found in Proverbs Chapter 5, 6, 7 along with other Scriptures) to get biblical insight on what I had fallen into.

After reading this I was immediately awakened to the reality of my terrible sin and what my consequences could be. I was lost and afraid of losing my wife and family, but yet knew deep in my heart I was determined somehow to fight to save my marriage. My friend gave me the phone number to his minister who in turn referred us to a marriage counselor who helped us through our marriage's most challenging times.

My advice for men who are now committing adultery is to stop and run from it right away. Cut it off fast and with reckless abandon for this becomes your first major step toward getting back on God's track. If you're thinking about having an adulterous affair, then totally abandon those thoughts and do not act upon them. Your best solution is to not start something that can so clearly destroy you and your spouses and family. Your next step should be to start reading and absorbing God's Word in the Bible regarding this area daily. Study, cling to and meditate on God's Word and it will help you change your life! In time I was able to confess my sins, start the process of repentance and asked God to take up residence in me. This would come in the form of the Holy Spirit, our counselor and guide. Galatians 5:16-17 reads: *So I say, live by the spirit and you will not gratify the desires of the sinful nature. For the sinful nature desires what is contrary to the Spirit and the Spirit what is contrary to the sinful nature.* My next step was to get rid of all old friends, acquaintances, places, habits, and any visuals that could lead me back to a life of sexual sin. This required a lot of patience, a persistent willingness to be transparent and honest with myself and with my wife. It took rejecting and rethinking what the 'Men's Code" had so strongly implanted in me.

With behavioral actions come consequences for us to face. Some of mine were that it would take two years of counseling to help repair our marriage. It would take much time and effort for me to regain my wife's forgiveness and trust. It would also take much time for me to rehabilitate my thinking and to take the proper actions on becoming a better husband, father and a better man. It would take years for me to rid myself of guilt and to forgive myself for what I had done. God greatly slowed down my career activities, and took away much of what I put value into. Now I understand that He did this to clean me up from the inside and to have me depend on Him, not my abilities and worldly accomplishments. I had lost a lot of time from my family and career by being off God's path. In Randy Alcorn's written journal titled "Deterring Immorality by Counting It's Cost, The exorbitant price of sexual sin" (see entire text in the appendix section of this book), he asked a former Christian leader who had fallen from committing adultery, "What could have been done to prevent this?" His answer was "If only I had really known, really thought through and weighed what it would cost me and my family and my Lord, I honestly believe I would never have done it." This is a powerful statement that we can use and frequently incorporate into our thinking. I'm most grateful that through God's grace and love, I was able to keep my wife and family together through this ordeal. My wife says that it was my unwavering willingness to do what ever it took to fight for our family that gave her the hope that we could repair and restore our marriage. God can and still works miracles in our lives! When seemingly the worst has happened, and we are without word, deed or power to fix it, God can work in and through our lives to have His will be done.

Bible Study-Chapter 16

Exodus 20:14 Do not commit adultery (Ten Commandments #8)

Matthew 5:27-28 (27) "You have heard that the law of Moses says, "Do not commit adultery." (28) "But I say, anyone who even looks at a woman with lust in his eye has already committed adultery in his heart."

Proverbs 2:16-20 Wisdom will save you from the immoral woman, from the seductive words of the promiscuous woman. (17) She has abandoned her husband and ignores the covenant she made before God. (18) Entering her house leads to death; it is the road to the grave. (19) The man who visits her is doomed. He will never reach the paths of life. (20) Follow the steps of good men instead, and stay on the paths of the righteous. NLT

Proverbs 5 (1) My son, pay attention to my wisdom, listen carefully to my wise counsel. (2) Then you will learn to be discreet and will store up knowledge. (3) The lips of an immoral woman are as sweet as honey, and her mouth is smoother than oil. (4) But the result is as bitter as poison, sharp as a double-edged sword. (5) Her feet go down to death; her steps lead straight to the grave. (6) For she does not care about the path to life. She staggers down a crooked trail and doesn't even realize where it leads. (7) so now my sons, listen to me. Never stray from what I'm about to say. (8) Run from her! Don't go near the door of her house! (9) If you do you will lose your honor and hand over to merciless people everything you have achieved in life. (10) Strangers will obtain your wealth, and someone else will enjoy the fruit of your labor. (11) Afterward you will groan in anguish when disease consumes your body, (12) and you will say, "How I hated discipline! If only I had not demanded my own way. (13) Oh why didn't I listen to my teachers? Why didn't I pay attention to those who gave me instruction? (14) I have come to the brink of utter ruin, and now I must face public disgrace." (15) Drink water from your own well share your love only with your wife. (16) Why spill the water of your springs in public, having sex with just anyone? (17) You should reserve it for yourselves. Don't share it with strangers. (18) Let your wife be a fountain of blessing for you. Rejoice in the wife of your youth! (19) Let her breasts satisfy you always. May you always be captivated by her love. (20) Why be captivated, my son with an immoral woman, or embrace the breast of an adulterous woman? (21) For the Lord sees clearly what a man does, examining every path he takes. (22) An evil man is held captive by his own sins; they are ropes that catch and hold him. (23) He will die for lack of self-control; he will be lost because of his incredible folly.

Proverbs 6:24-32 (24) These commands and this teaching will keep you from the immoral woman, from the smooth tongue of an adulterous woman. (25) Don't lust after her beauty. Don't let her coyness seduce you. (26) For a prostitute will bring you to poverty, and sleeping with another man's wife may cost you your very life. (27) Can a man scoop fire into his lap and not be burned? Can he not walk on hot coals and not blister his feet? (29) So is it with the man who sleeps with another man's wife. He who embraces her will not go unpunished. (32) But the man who commits adultery is an utter fool, for he destroys his own soul. (33) Wounds and constant disgrace are his lot. His shame will never be erased. (34) For the woman's husband will be furious in his jealousy, and he will have no mercy in his days of vengeance. (35) There is no compensation or bribe that will satisfy him.

Proverbs 7 (1) Follow my advice, my son, always treasure my commands. (2) Obey them and live! Guard my teachings as your most precious possession. (3) Tie them on your fingers as a reminder. Write them deep within your heart. (4) Love wisdom like a sister; make insight a beloved member of your family. (5) Let them hold you back from an affair with an adulterous woman, from listening to the flattery of an adulterous woman. (6) I was looking out the window of my house one day (7) and saw a simpleminded young man who lacked common sense. (8) He was crossing the street near the house of an immoral woman. He was strolling down the path by her house (9) at twilight, as the day was fading, as the dark of night set in. (10) The woman approached him, dressed seductively and sly of heart. (11) She was the brash, rebellious type who never stays at home. (12) She is often seen in the streets and markets soliciting at every corner. (13) She threw her arms around him and kissed him, and with a brazen look she said, (14) "I've offered my sacrifices and just finished my vows. (15) It's you I was looking for! I came out to find you, and here you are! (16) My bed is covered with colored sheets of finest linens imported from Egypt. (17) I perfumed my bed with myrrh, aloes and cinnamon. (18) Come, let's drink our fill of love until morning. Let's enjoy each other's caresses, (19) for my husband is not home. He's away on a long trip. (20) He has taken a wallet full of money with him and he won't return until the end of the month. (21) So she seduced him with her pretty speech. With her flattery she enticed him. (22) He followed her at once, like an ox going to the slaughter or like a trapped stag. (23) awaiting the arrow that would pierce its heart. He was like a bird flying into the snare, little knowing it would cost him his life. (24) Listen to me my sons and pay attention to my words. (25) Don't let your hearts stray away toward her. Don't wander down her wayward path. 26) for she has been the ruin of many;

numerous men have been her victims. (27) Her house is the road to the grave. Her bedroom is the den of death.

Proverbs 23:27-28 (27) A prostitute is a deep pit and a wayward wife is a narrow well.

(28) Like a bandit she lies in wait and multiples the unfaithful among men. (NIV)

Deuteronomy 22:22 If a man is discovered committing adultery, both he and the other man's wife must be killed. In this way, the evil will be cleansed from Israel.

Romans 7:2-3 (2) Let me illustrate. When a woman marries, the law binds her to her husband as long as he is alive. But if he dies, the laws of marriage no longer apply to her. (3) So while her husband is alive, she would be committing adultery if she married another man. But if her husband dies, she is free from the law and does not commit adultery when she remarries.

James 4:4 "You adulterers! Don't you realize that friendship with this world makes you an enemy of God? I say it again that, if your aim is to enjoy this world, you can't be a friend of God.

David and Bathsheba's Adulterous Affair

2 Samuel 11 Highlights other sins including coveting neighbors wife, murder, deceit and false witness against neighbor. (1) The following spring, the time of year when kings go to war, David sent Joab and the Israelite army to destroy the Ammonites. In the process, they laid siege to the city of Rabbath. But David stayed behind in Jerusalem. (2) Late one afternoon David got out of bed after taking a nap and went for a stroll on the roof of the palace. As he looked out over the city, he noticed a woman of unusual beauty taking a bath. (3) He sent someone to find out who she was, and he was told, "She is Bathsheba, the daughter of Eliam and the wife of Uriah the Hittite." (4) Then David sent for her; and she came to the palace, he slept with her. (She had just completed the purification rites after having her menstrual period). Then she returned home. (5) Later when Bathsheba discovered that she was pregnant, she sent a message to inform David. (6) So David sent word to Joab: 'Send me Uriah the Hittite." (7) When Uriah arrived,

David asked him how Joab and the army were getting along and how the war was progressing. (8) Then he told Uriah, "Go on home and relax." David even sent a gift to Uriah, after he had left the palace. (9) But Uriah wouldn't go home. He stayed that night at the palace entrance with some of the king's other servants. (10) When David heard what Uriah had done, he summoned him and asked, "What's the matter with you? Why didn't you go home last night after being away for so long? (11) Uriah replied, " The Ark and the armies of Israel and Judah are living in tents, and Joab and his officers are camping in the open fields. How could I go home to wine and dine and sleep with my wife? I swear I will never be guilty of acting like that." (12) "Well stay here tonight," David told him, " and tomorrow you may return to the army." So Uriah stayed in Jerusalem that day and the next. (13) Then David invited him to dinner and got him drunk. But even then he couldn't get Uriah to go home to his wife. Again he slept at the palace entrance. (14) So the next morning David wrote a letter to Joab and gave it to Uriah to deliver. (15) The letter instructed Joab, "Station Uriah on the front lines where the battle is fiercest. Then pull back so that he will be killed" (16) So Joab assigned Uriah to a spot close to the city wall where he knew the enemies strongest men were fighting. (17) And Uriah was killed along with several other Israelite soldiers. (18) Then Joab sent a battle report to David. (19) He told his messenger, "Report all the news of the battle to the king. (20) But he might get angry and ask, "Why did the troops go so close to the city? Didn't they know there would be shooting from the walls? (21) Wasn't Gideon's son Abimelech killed at Thebez by a woman who threw a millstone down on him? Then tell him, Uriah the Hittie was killed too" (22) So the messenger went to Jerusalem and gave a complete report to David. (23) "The enemy came out against us," he said. "And as we chased them back to the city gates, (24) the archers on the wall shot arrows at us. Some of our men were killed including Uriah the Hittie. (25) "Well, tell Joab not to be discouraged," David said. "The sword kills one as well as the other! Fight harder next time, and conquer the city!" (26) When Bathsheba heard that her husband was dead, she mourned for him. (27) When the period of mourning was over, David sent for her and bought her to the palace, and she became one of his wives. Then she gave birth to a son. But the Lord was very displeased with what David had done.

God's anger and consequences for David

2 Samuel 12:1-12 (1) So the Lord sent Nathan the prophet to tell David this story: "There were two men in a certain town. One was rich, and one was poor. (2) the rich man owned sheep and cattle. (3) The poor man owned nothing but a little lamb he had worked hard to buy. He raised that little lamb, and it grew up with his children. It ate from the man's own plate and drank from it's cup. He cuddled it in his arms like a baby daughter. (4) One day a guest arrived at the home of the rich man. But instead of killing a lamb from his own flocks for food, he took the poor man's lamb and killed it and served it to his guest." (5) David was furious. "As surely as the Lord lives" he vowed, "any man who would do such a thing deserves to die! (6) He must repay four lambs to the poor man for the one he stole and for having no pity." (7) Then Nathan said to David, "You are that man! The Lord, the God of Israel says, I anointed you king of Israel and saved you from the power of Saul. (8) I gave you his house and his wives and the kingdoms of Israel and Judah. And if that had not been enough, I would have given you much, much more. (9) Why then have you despised the word of the Lord and done this horrible deed? For you have murdered Uriah and stolen his wife. (10) From this time on, the sword will be a constant threat to your family, because you have despised me by taking Uriah's wife to be your own. (11) "Because of what you have done, I, the Lord, will cause your household to rebel against you. I will give your wives to another man, and he will go to bed with them in public view. (12) You did it secretly but I will do this to you openly in the sight of all Israel."

David's Confession of Guilt

2 Samuel 12:13-25 (13) Then David confessed to Nathan (the prophet), "I have sinned against the Lord." Nathan replied, "Yes, but the Lord has forgiven you, and you won't die for this sin. (14) But you have given the enemies of the Lord great opportunity to despise and blaspheme him, so your child will die." (15) After Nathan returned to his home, the Lord made Bathsheba's baby deathly ill. (16) David begged God to spare the child. He went without food and lay all night on the bare ground. (17) The leaders of the nation pleaded with him to get up and eat with them, but he refused. (18) Then on the seventh day the baby died. David's advisers were afraid to tell him. "He was so broken up about the baby being sick," they said. "What will he do to himself when we tell him the child is dead?" (19) But when David saw them whispering, he realized what had happened. "Is the baby dead?" he asked. "Yes," they replied. (20) Then David got up from the ground, washed himself, put on lotions, and changed his clothes. Then he went to the Tabernacle and worshiped the Lord. After that, he returned to the palace and ate. (21) His advisers were amazed, "we don't understand you", they told him. "While the baby was still living, you wept and refused to eat. But now that the baby is dead, you have stopped your mourning and are eating again." (22) David replied, "I fasted and wept while the child was alive, for I said, Perhaps the Lord will be gracious to me and let the child live. (23) But why should I fast when he is dead? Can I bring him back again? I will go to him one day, but he cannot return to me. (24) Then David confronted Bathsheba, his wife, and slept with her. She became pregnant and gave birth to a son, and they named him Solomon. The Lord loved the child (25) and sent word through Nathan, the prophet, that his name should be Jedidiah, "beloved of the Lord", because the Lord loved him.

Study Application Notes

Matthew 5:27-28 The Old Testament law said that it is wrong for a person to have sex with someone other than his or her spouse (*Exodus 20:14*). But Jesus said that the desire to have sex with someone other than your spouse is mental   adultery and thus sin. Jesus emphasized that if the act is wrong, then so is the intention. To be faithful to your spouse with your body but not your mind is to break the trust so vital to a strong marriage. Jesus is not condemning natural interest in the opposite sex or even healthy sexual desire, but the deliberate and repeated filling of one's mind with fantasies that would be evil if acted out.

Matthew 5:27-28 Acting out lustful desires is harmful in several ways; (1) it causes people to excuse sin rather than to stop sinning; (2) it destroys marriages: (3) it is a deliberate rebellion against God's word; (4) it always hurts someone else in addition to the sinner (children, family members and friends). Sinful action is more dangerous than sinful desire and that's why sinful desires should not be acted out. Nevertheless, sinful desire is just as damaging to righteousness. Left unchecked, wrong desires will result in wrong actions and turn people away from God.

Proverbs 5:3 This "adulteress" is a prostitute. Proverbs includes many warnings against illicit sex for several reasons. First a prostitute's charm is used as an example of any temptation to do wrong or to leave the pursuit of wisdom. Second, sexual immorality of any kind was and still is extremely dangerous. It destroys family life. It erodes a person's ability to love. It degrades human beings and turns them into objects. It can lead to disease. It can result in unwanted children. Third, sexual immorality is against God's law.

Proverbs 5:3-8 Any person should be on guard against those who use flattery and smooth speech (lips that drip honey) that would lead him or her into sin. The best advice is to take a detour and even avoid conversation with such people.

Proverbs 5:11-13 At the end of your life it will be too late to ask for advice. When desire is fully activated, people don't want advice-they want satisfaction. The best time to learn the dangers and foolishness of going after forbidden sex (or anything else that is harmful) is long before the temptation comes. Resistance is easier if the decision has already been made. Don't wait to see what happens, prepare for temptation by deciding now how you will act when you face it.

Proverbs 5:15 "Drink water from your own cistern" is a picture of faithfulness in a marriage. It means to enjoy the spouse God has given you.

Proverbs 5:15-21 In contrast to much of what we read, see and hear today this passage urges couples to look to each other for lifelong satisfaction and companionship. Many temptations entice husbands and wives to desert each other for excitement and pleasures to be found elsewhere when marriage becomes dull. But God designed marriage and sanctified it and only within this covenant relationship can we find real love and fulfillment. Don't let God's best for you be wasted on illusions of greener pastures somewhere else. Instead rejoice with your spouse as you give yourself to God and to each other.

Proverbs 5:18-20 God does not intend faithfulness in marriage to be boring, lifeless, pleasureless, and dull. Sex is a gift God gives to married people for their mutual enjoyment. Real happiness comes when we decide to find pleasure in the relationship God has given us and to commit ourselves to making it pleasurable for our spouse. The real danger is in doubting that God cares for us. We then may resent his timing and carelessly pursue sexual pleasure without his blessing.

Proverbs 6:25 Regard lust as a warning sign of danger ahead. When you notice that you are attracted to a person of the opposite sex or preoccupied with thoughts of him or her, your desires may lead you to sin, Ask God to help you change your desires before you are drawn into sin.

Proverbs 6:25-30 Some people argue that it is all right to break God's law against sexual sin if nobody gets hurt. In truth, somebody always gets hurt. Spouses are devastated and children are scared. The partners themselves, even if they escape disease and unwanted pregnancy, lose their ability to fulfill commitments, to feel sexual desire, to trust, and to be entirely open with another person. God's laws are not arbitrary. They do not forbid good clean fun, rather they warn us against destroying ourselves through unwise actions or running ahead of God's timetable.

Proverbs 7:25-27 You can take definite steps to avoid sexual sins. First, guard your mind. Don't read books, look at pictures, or encourage fantasies that simulate the wrong desires. Second, keep away from settings and friends that tempt you to sin. Third, don't think only of the moment, focus on the future. Today's thrill may lead to tomorrow's ruin.

Proverbs 23:27-28 Three thousand years later after this proverb was written hasn't changed the fact that illicit sex is one of the most alluring and destructive enticements. It promise pleasure and escape from our troubles, but in the end it release a poison of shame and embarrassment. The only real solution for our problems is Jesus Christ. When we surrender our lives to him and turn from our sins, we are free to live Godly and fulfilling lives. The temptations will still be here, but now we have God working with us to help us resist them. He will help us to grow and mature in our spiritual walk.

James 4:4 Having a friendship with the world involves seeking pleasure at other's expense or at the expense of obeying God. Pleasure that keeps us from pleasing God is sinful; pleasure from God's rich bounty is good.

2 *Samuel 11:1-5* David choose to stay at home and rest instead of leading his men into battle. That was his first mistake. Then, on a sleepless night, the king saw Bathsheba bathing on a nearby rooftop. David didn't have to watch her, he choose to do so. After indulging his visual lust, David gratified his sexual desire. He fell into the sin of adultery. It is the idle times in life that frequently gets us into trouble. Staying busy with healthy activities can do much to protect us from temptation. We are also reminded to diligently guard what we allow ourselves to watch or think about. Failure in our thought life will usually lead to a fall.

2 *Samuel 11:1-17* In this episode of Bathsheba, David allowed himself to fall deeper and deeper into sin. (1) David abandoned his purpose by staying at home from war (11:1). (2) He focused on his own desires (11:3). (3) When temptation came, he look into it instead of turning away from it (11:4). (4) He sinned deliberately (11:4). (5) He tried to cover up his sins by deceiving others (11:6-15). (6) He committed murder to continue the cover-up (11:15-17). Eventually, David's sin was exposed (12:9). (7) The consequences of David's sin were far-reaching affecting many others (11:17, 12:11,14, 15). David could have chosen to stop and turn from evil at any stage along the way. But once sin gets started, it is difficult to stop. The deeper the mess, the less we want to admit having caused it. It's much easier to stop sliding down a hill when you are near the top than when you are half way down. The best solution is to stop sin before it starts.

2 *Samuel 11:3-4* To flee temptation (1) Ask God in earnest prayer to help you stay away from people, places and situations that may tempt you. (2) Memorize and meditate on portions of Scripture that combat your specific weaknesses. (3) Find another believer whom you can openly share your struggles, and call this person for help when temptation strikes.

2 *Samuel 11:25* David's response to Uriah's death seemed flippant and insensitive. While he grieved deeply for Saul and Abner, his rivals (chapter 1:31-39) he showed no grief for Uriah, a good man with strong spiritual character. Why? David had become callous to his own sin. The only way he could cover up his first sin (adultery) was to sin again, and soon he no longer felt guilty for what he had done. Feelings are not reliable guides for determining right and wrong. Deliberate repeated sinning had dulled David's sensitivity to God's laws and others rights. The more you try to cover-up a sin the more insensitive you become toward it. Don't become hardened to sin as David did. Confess your wrong actions to God before you forget they are sins.

11:14-17 Since Uriah refused to sleep with his wife, which would have covered for Bathsheba's adulterous pregnancy, David engineered his death. One hidden sin almost always leads to another. Only when we confess our sins, bringing them out into the open can we be free of the destructive cycle. Confession involves admitting our wrongs to God, ourselves and another person. This is an important key to breaking free from our past failures.

2 Samuel 12:1-7 God choose his prophet Nathan to intervene after David's failure. Notice how Nathan used a story to broach the topic with David. Then, when David had become emotionally involved, Nathan turned to direct confrontation: "You are that man!" Nathan hoped that this piercing declaration would help David realize the serious nature of his sin and bring him to repentance. Nathan's wise intervention should serve as a model for us. He confronted David with the terrible reality of his acts, but he did it in such a way that David would listen. When you have to confront someone with unpleasant news, pray for courage, skill and tact. If you want that person to respond constructively, think through what you are going to say. How you present your message may be just as important as what you say. Part of our spiritual growth calls us to participate in the spiritual growth of others. There may be times when God will use us to help someone else see the truth of their spiritual condition.

12:9-13 David's admission here, "I have sinned against the Lord" was the right response to his wrongdoing. Spurred by Nathan's appeal, it was an acknowledgement of David's accountability before God. He saw truth, confessed his sin, accepted responsibility for his actions, grieved before the Lord, and pleaded with God to cleanse his heart and set him on the right course. (Psalm 51). Notice, however, that despite David's humble confession, he would still have to face terrible consequences. Our confession only starts the process toward a new life; we still must face the consequences of our past actions. But we can be sure as we build for a productive future, God will help us with the difficulties arising from our past.

12:13 During this incident, David wrote Psalms 51, giving valuable insight into his character and offering hope for us as well. No matter how miserable guilt makes you feel or how terrible you have sinned, you can pour out your heart to God and seek his forgiveness as David did. There is God's forgiveness for us when we sin!

12:14 David confessed and repented in his sins, but God's judgment was that his child would die. The consequences of David's sin were irreversible. Sometimes an apology isn't enough. When God forgives us and restores our relationship with him, he doesn't eliminate all the consequences of our wrongdoing. We may be tempted to say, "If this is wrong, I can always apologize to God", but we must remember that we may set into motion events with irreversible consequences.

12:14 Why did the child have to die? This was not a judgment on the child for being conceived out of wedlock, but a judgment on David for his sin. David and Bathsheba deserved to die, but God sparred their lives and took the child instead. God still had work for David to do in building the kingdom. The child's death was tragic and also a terrible punishment for David and Bathsheba to bear. Does God reward murder and adultery by giving a king a new heir? While God readily forgave David's sin, he did not negate all it's consequence.

12:20-24 David did not continue to dwell on his sin. He returned to God and God forgave him, opening the way to begin life anew. Even the name God gave Solomon (Jedidiah, "loved by the Lord") was a reminder of God's grace. When we return to God, accept his forgiveness, and change our ways, he gives us a fresh start. To feel forgiven as David did, admit your sins to god and turn to him. Then move ahead with a new and fresh approach to life.

Self Reflection

1. How does this topic apply to me?

2. What truths in this area do I recognize and how can I fully address them?

3. What Bible verses here best encourage and inspire me to want to be a better husband, father and a better man in this area?

4. What steps can I begin to take today to strengthen myself in this area?

5. Who can I reach out to for personal help and support in this area? (This could be a family member, friend, professional counselor, a spiritual leader or someone you worship with)

Journal

Journal

17. God's Forgiveness and Healing

God is big on forgiveness and he is quick to show mercy much like a father who forgives his child for doing something wrong. After realizing the extent of the hurt and damage I caused my wife and family, I became very ashamed of my behavior and questioned how could I do such a hurtful and sinful deed against God and my family. With some thought the answer became obvious, I allowed sin to separate me from God choosing to be unfaithful to my wife and family. But through God's strength, I would choose to repent that sin and begin to live a completely changed life. No more would I give in and let the "Men's Code" be my guide. God's forgiveness and grace to me was huge, in fact it was nothing short of a miracle. He allowed our marriage to stay together, although it was extremely challenging and difficult. First, God soften both my wife's and my heart to be open and receptive to his healing and forgiveness. Second, over time he was able to renew and restore our marriage in many respects better than it was before. Third, God was able to keep our children from becoming directly involved thus allowing our family to not have to suffer deep emotional scars. Fourth, God birthed us more time together by taking me away from the traps in my career. Fifth, God did not take away my talents and gifts.

God's forgiveness allowed me to have a season of healing, restoration renewing and rebuilding. It's amazing how God took our terribly bad situation and was able to use it to show others that through him alone a marriage in trouble can become a marriage restored and healed! Psalms 103:2 sums up my feeling for what the Lord has done in my life, *"Praise the Lord I tell myself and never forget the good things he does for me."* God's love and healing is available to anyone who's heart is willing to listen to the him, turn from their sins and to start obeying his loving words. Through God's forgiveness and healing, I'm now able to give praise, honor and glory to God by sharing my testimony with others. If God can work in and through me, he can do the same for you. I knew God's forgiveness was in full effect by the way he allowed my wife and marriage counselor to begin working positively through out and with in me. It required that I participate by demonstrating a strong desire to hear and begin applying God's word in my life. Through daily Bible reading, prayer and meditation I began the process of aligning my thoughts with the Lord's. This was a new way of thinking and didn't happen over night but I was quick to dive in sincerely into God's calling.

Then I had to come to terms with forgiving myself. This sounds simple but it wasn't. I was filled with tremendous guilt for a long time. Yes it's true that although I wasn't filled with guilt while being unfaithful, I took full responsibility for my behavior. As God began to let the seeds of forgiveness take root in our marriage, I would come to understand that I was free from the bondage of my previous sins. This is when I was able to forgive myself.

Bible Study-Chapter 17

John 8:1-11 (1) Jesus returned to the Mount of Olives, (2) but early the next morning he was back again at the Temple. A crowd soon gathered and he sat down and taught them. (3) As he was speaking, the teachers of religious law and Pharisees brought a woman they had caught in the act of adultery. (4) "Teacher," they said to Jesus, " this woman was caught in the very act of adultery. (5) The law of Moses says to stone her! What do you say?" (6) They were trying to trap him into saying something they could use against him, but Jesus stooped down and wrote in the dust with his finger. (7) They kept demanding an answer, so he stood up again and said "All right stone her. But let those who have never sinned throw the first stones". (8) Then he stooped down again and wrote in the dust. (9) When the accusers heard this, they slipped away one by one, beginning with the oldest, until only Jesus was left in the middle of the crowd with the woman. (10) Then Jesus stood up again and said to her, "Where are your accusers"? Didn't even one of them condemn you? (11) "No Lord," she said. And Jesus said, "Neither do I, Go and sin no more."

Luke 15:3-10 (3) So Jesus used this illustration: (4) "If you had one hundred sheep, and one of them strayed away and was lost in the wilderness, wouldn't you leave the ninety nine others to go and search for the lost one until you found it? (5) And then you would joyfully carry it home on your shoulders. (6) When you arrived, you would call together your friends and neighbors to rejoice with you because your lost sheep was found. (7) In the same way, heaven will be happier over one lost sinner who returns to God than over ninety-nine others who are righteous and haven't strayed away. (8) Or suppose a woman had ten valuable silver coins and loses one. Won't she light a lamp and look in every corner of the house and sweep every nook and cranny until she finds it? (9) And when she finds it, she will call her friends and neighbors to rejoice with her because she has found her lost coin. (10) In the same way, there is joy in the presence of God's angels when even one sinner repents."

2 *Samuel* 14:14 All of us must die eventually. Our lives are like water spilled out on the ground, which cannot be gathered up again. That is why God tries to bring us back when we have been separated from him. He does not sweep away the lives of those he cares about, and neither should you!

***Psalms* 32** (1) Oh, what joy for those whose rebellion is forgiven, whose sin is put out of sight! (2) Yes, what joy for those whose record the Lord has cleared of sin, whose lives are lived in complete honesty! (3) When I refused to confess my sin, I was weak and miserable, and I groaned all day long. (4) Day and night your hand of discipline was heavy on me. My strength evaporated like water in the summer heat. (5) Finally, I confessed all my sins to you and stopped trying hide them. I said to myself, "I will confess my rebellion to the lord" And you forgave me! All my guilt is gone. (6) Therefore, let all the Godly confess their rebellion to you while there is time, that they may not drown in the floodwaters of judgment. (7) For you are my hiding place; you protect me from trouble, you surround me with songs of victory. (8) The Lord says, "I will guide you along the best pathway for your life. I will advise and watch over you. (9) Do not be like a senseless horse or mule that needs a bit and bridle to keep it under control" (10) Many sorrows come to the wicked, but unfailing love surrounds those who trust the Lord. (11) So rejoice in the Lord and be glad, all of you who obey him! Shout for joy, all you whose hearts are pure!

***Psalms* 103** Key *verses include* (1) Praise the Lord, I tell myself, with my whole heart, I will praise his Holy name. (2) Praise the Lord, I tell myself, and never forget the good things he does for me. (3) He forgives all my sins and heals all my diseases. (4) He ransoms me from death and surrounds me with love and tender mercies. (5) He fills my life with good things. My youth is renewed like the eagles! (7) He revealed his character to Moses and his deeds to the people of Israel. (8) The Lord is merciful and gracious; he is slow to get angry and full of unfailing love. (9) He will not constantly accuse us, nor remain angry forever. (10) He has not punished us for all our sins, nor does he deal with us as we deserve. (11) For his unfailing love toward those who fear him is as great as the height of the heavens above the earth. (12) He has removed our rebellious acts as far away from us as the east is from the west. (13) The Lord is like a father to his children, tender and compassionate to those who fear him. (14) For he understands how weak we are; he knows we are only dust. (15) Our days on earth are like grass, like wildflowers, we bloom and die. (16) The wind blows, and we are gone, as though we had never been here. (17) But the love of the Lord remains forever with those who fear him. His salvation extends to the children's children (18) of those who are faithful to his covenant of those who obey his commandments! (22) Praise the Lord, everything he has created, everywhere in his kingdom. As for me, I too, will praise the Lord.

1 *Peter* 5:10-11 (10) In his kindness God called you to his eternal glory by means of Jesus Christ. After you have suffered for a little while, he will restore, support and strengthen you, and he will place you on a firm foundation. (11) All power is his forever and ever, Amen.

2 *Corinthians* 5:14-15 What ever we do, it is because Christ's love controls us. Since we believe that Christ died for everyone, we also believe that we have all died to the old life we use to live. 15) He died for everyone so that those who receive his new life will no longer live to please themselves. Instead, they will live to please Christ, who died and was raised for them.

***Romans* 3:23** For all have sinned and fall short of the glory of God. *(NIV)*

Study Application Notes

John 8:3-6 The Jewish leaders had already disregarded the law by arresting the woman without the man. The law required that both parties to adultery be stoned (Leviticus 20:10, Deuteronomy 22:22) The leaders were using the woman as a trap so they could trick Jesus. If Jesus said the woman should not be stoned, they would accuse him of violating Moses' law. If he urged them to execute her, they would report him to the Romans, who did not permit the Jews to carry out their own executions.

8:7 This is a significant statement about judging others. Because Jesus upheld the legal penalty for adultery, stoning, he could not be accused of being against the law. But by saying that only a sinless person could throw the first stone, he highlighted the importance of compassion and forgiveness. When others are caught in sin, are you quick to pass judgment? To do so is to act as though you have never sinned. It is God's role to judge, not ours. Our role is to show forgiveness and compassion.

8:11 Jesus did not condemn the woman accused of adultery, but neither did he ignore or condone her sin. He told her to go and sin no more. He also forgave her and gave her a new start in life. Jesus stands ready to forgive any sin in your life, but confession and repentance mean a change of heart. With God's help we can accept Christ's forgiveness and stop our wrongdoing.

Luke 15:3-10 The stories of the lost sheep and lost coin show God's grace toward those who have strayed and his great joy in finding them. Though our past may be tarnished, we are extremely valuable in the eyes of God. This value is reflected in the symbolism of the coin and sheep (valuable commodities in that day). The fact that the owner would stop every thing else to search for the one lost shows even more how valuable we are to the one who owns us.

Psalms 32:1-4 Making restitution for our past failures and reconciling our relationships is an important part of our spiritual growth. We see in this psalm that we suffer unnecessary guilt by refusing to confess our sin. As David declared, we can know great joy when we receive forgiveness for our sins.

32:5-9 Like David, we need to confess our sins before God and receive forgiveness. When we do so, we also set a good example for others who are having a hard time admitting their sin to God. We also set our hearts free from the destructive grip of guilt and restore our relationship with God. Then we can learn to live in obedience to the Lord's will and respond willingly to his instruction.

32:5 What is confession? To confess our sin is to agree with God, acknowledging that he is right to declare what we have done as sinful, and that we are wrong to desire or to do it. It means affirming our intention of abandoning that that sin in order to follow God more faithfully. (NIV)

Psalms 103:1-6 David's praise focused on the good things God was doing for him. It is easy to complain about life, but David's list gives us plenty for which to praise God. He forgives our sins, heals our diseases, redeems us from death, crowns us with love and compassion, satisfies our desires, and gives righteousness and justice. We receive all of these without deserving any of them. No matter how difficult your life's journey, you can always count your blessings, past, present and future. When you feel as though you have nothing to praise God, read David's list. (NIV)

103:7 God's law was first given to Moses and the people of Israel. God's law presents a clear picture of God's character and will for his people. It was God's training manual to prepare his people to serve him to follow his ways. Review the ten commandments (Exodus 20) and the history on how they were given, asking God to show you his will and his ways through them. (NIV)

103:8-12 David praised God for his great love and kindness. We have all failed and our mistakes have hurt other people and damaged or destroyed our relationships. Sometimes others have a hard time forgiving us, even when we seek to make restitution. God, on the other hand, is waiting to forgive us. All we have to do is to admit our sin and surrender our lives to him.

103:12 East and west can never meet. This is a symbolic portrait of God's forgiveness, when he forgives our sin, he separates it from us and doesn't even remember it. We need never to wallow in the past, for God forgives and forgets. We tend to dredge up the ugly past, but God has wiped our record clean. If we are to follow God, we must model his forgiveness. When we forgive another, we must also forgive the sin. Otherwise, we have not truly forgiven. (NIV) This should be very encouraging to us!

103:13-18 In the same manner that a loving father cares about his children, God has compassion on all who call on him. God's love never ceases and we can be assured that he will be faithful to all his promises to us.

1 *Peter* 5:10-11 God's promise to us when we fall down or are pushed down is that he will pick us up, set us in a good and secure place, and use the difficulty we have been through to make us stronger than ever! It is this hope that gives us the courage to persevere in our spiritual journeys.

2 *Corinthians* 5:14-15 Everything that Paul and his companions did was to honor God. Not only did fear of God motivate them, but Christ's love compelled their actions. The word for "compels" means "to hold fast." In other words, the love of Christ was constraining them to certain courses of action. They knew that Jesus, out of his great love, had given up his life for their sakes. He had not acted out of his own self–interest, selfishly holding on to the glory of heaven that he already possessed. Instead, Jesus had willing "died for all." Because Christ died for us, we are dead to our old lives. Like Paul, we should no longer live to please our selves, we should spend our lives pleasing Christ.

Romans 3:23 All sin makes us sinners and cuts us off from God. Don't minimize certain sins for other. All sin can be forgiven.

Self Reflection

1. How does this topic apply to me?

2. What truths in this area can I recognize and how can I fully address them?

3. What Bible verses here best encourage and inspire me to want to be a better husband, father and a better man in this area?

4. What steps can I begin to take today to strengthen myself in this area?

5. Who can I reach out to for personal help and support in this area? (This could be a family member, friend, professional counselor, a spiritual leader or someone you worship with)

Journal

18. Making Choices, Making Changes

To begin our quest on becoming a "Virtuous Man" we have to start immediately making choices and changes in our lives. These must completely be in line with God's Code as is revealed in the Bible. It means giving up old ways of how we think, act and the habits associated with them and begin exercising sound judgment over our impulses. Particularly how it relates to our relationship with God, our spouse, and family. We now choose no longer to have our lives controlled and ultimately destroyed by the "Men's Code" and the sins it encourages us to indulge in. We are now free through God's power to choose, embrace and live our lives through God's Code. The code of love, faithfulness, righteousness, reverence, and obedience to God. For me, breaking the "Men's Code" was a process of rejecting it on a step-by-step basis. Examining each of its components and choosing to resist and replace them through study, acceptance and application of God's loving Words.

My first step was to recognize that I needed to make important and major changes in my life. I could no longer live and act foolishly and in a selfish manner. I knew that this was not going to be easy and would require much faith, trust, and patience that God would somehow work out a very difficult situation. I made the choice to begin at once to start living for God, my wife and family, putting them first in that same order. Secondly I made the choice to continue getting the help I needed. This was accomplished through. (a) my willing, persistent commitment to attend counseling for a period of two years both with my wife and on an individual basis, (b) started attending a Bible teaching Church on a regular basis, (c) reading and studying the Bible on a daily basis 1-2 hours each day, (d) daily prayer, mediation and quiet time, (e) distanced and removed myself from any past friends, associations, activities or places that where in any way connected to my past life of sin. (f) reached out to old friends and new friends that God had put next to me who were good strong Godly men. People who were a good example of walking the walk, who openly lived Godly lives and would hold me accountable as well. At some point in this process, I became moved by the Holy Spirit to want to write down Bible verses I read which encouraged, inspired, and directed me to begin living this changed life in Christ. All of these Scriptures became the basis of this "Men's Biblical Manual." Perhaps the biggest choice and change for me was when I decided it was time to give my entire life back to Christ and got baptized! This happened about two and a half years into our process.

I remember my wife asking me to make sure that I was sincere about my actions and I assured not only her, but God that my heart was in the right place. I wanted every area of my life to be in harmony and on the path of God's will and no longer my will. It is to be noted that I was baptized at age eight but had gotten away from living as God directs us to as I grew older. Then at age fifty-one God got my attention once again in a huge way and this time I knew it was time to come back to his flock. The other important part of this chapter involves making the choice to remain consistent in my new walk and continue on a daily and moment to moment basis. I now know that how I use to live my life is something that I can and will never return to. I now have God's Code firmly in my heart, mind, body, and soul and have defeated Satan through God's power, promises, and omnipresence in my life. Proverbs 23:26 says *"My son, give me your heart and let your eye keep to my ways."* Do situations or thoughts arise that bring up tempting urges? Yes they do at times, but I'm now clothed with the tools, thoughts, new habits, Godly people in my life and the Holy Spirit in me to resist, turn away from and continue to walk on level, blameless paths. Our marriage counselor recommended a book that was extremely useful. "How To Love A Black Woman" by Dr. Ronn Elmore. It is good supplemental reading that enlightens men on what women say they need and want from men. It explains those issues with constructive, practical, simple and concise ways that men can apply in there marriages. Do not be mislead by the book's title and think this only applies to black people. It could have also been titled "How To Love A Woman" because it reveals universal truths and situations that relate to men and woman of all ethnicities.

My wife continues to say that next to my seeking and honoring God now in my life, that doing the work of repentance gave her new faith in me to want to work at saving and restoring our marriage. Next to God, she has been my biggest encouragement, and inspiration to continue to grow in God's character and love. My children fuel me the hope that I can be their best example of how to change ones life when faced with difficult situations in their lives. It is my hope that they will learn vicariously through them on what and how to avoid what mom and dad went through. Romans 8:28 sums up best what God did during our marriage crises.... *"And we know that in all things God works for the good of those who love him, who have been called accordingly to his purpose."* The following verses are beautiful and continue to inspire and instruct me on how to become "The Virtuous Man."

Bible Study-Chapter 18

Psalms 51:1-17 (1) Have mercy on me, O God, because of your unfailing love. Because of your great compassion, blot out the stain of my sin. (2) Wash me clean from my guilt. Purify me from my sin. (3) For I recognize my shameful deeds, they haunt me day and night. (4) Against you, and you alone have I sinned; I've done what is evil in your sight. You will be proved right in what you say, and your judgment against me is just. (5) For I was born a sinner, yes from the moment my mother conceived me. (6) But you desire honesty from the heart, so you can teach me to be wise in my inmost being. (7) Purify me from my sins, and I will be clean; wash me, and I'll be whiter than snow. (8) Oh, give me back my joy again; you have broken me, now let me rejoice. (9) Don't keep looking at my sins. Remove the stain of my guilt. (10) Create in me a clean heart, O God. Renew a right spirit within me. (11) Do not banish me from your presence, and don't take your Holy Spirit from me. (12) Restore to me again the joy of your salvation, and make me willing to obey you. (13) Then I will teach your ways to sinners, and they will return to you. (14) Forgive me for shedding blood, O God who saves, then I will joyfully sing of your forgiveness. (15) Unseal my lips, O Lord, that I may praise you. (16) You would not be pleased with sacrifices or I would bring them. If I brought you a burnt offering, you would not accept it. (17) The sacrifice you want is a broken spirit, a broken and repentant heart. O God you will not despise.

Luke 18:10-14 (10) Two men went to the temple to pray. One was a Pharisee and the other was a dishonest tax collector. (11) The proud Pharisee stood by himself and prayed this prayer: 'I thank you, God that I am not a sinner, like everyone else, especially like that tax collector over there! For I never cheat, I don't sin, I don't commit adultery. (12) I fast twice a week and I give you a tenth of my income.' (13) But the tax collector stood at a distance and dared not to lift his eyes to heaven as he prayed. Instead he beat his chest in sorrow saying, 'O God be merciful to me for I am a sinner.' (14) I tell you this sinner, not the Pharisee, will return home justified before God. For the proud will be humbled, but the humble will be honored."

John 1:8-9 If we say we have no sin, we are only fooling ourselves and refusing to accept the truth. (9) But if we confess our sins to him, he is faithful and just to forgive us from every wrong.

Proverbs 28:13 People who cover over their sins will not prosper. But if they confess and forsake them, they will receive mercy.

Proverbs 3:5-7 Trust in the Lord with all of your heart, do not depend on your own understanding. (6) Seek his will in all that you do, and he will direct your paths. (7) Don't be impressed with your own wisdom. Instead fear the Lord and turn your back on evil.

Proverbs 29:3 The man who loves wisdom brings joy to his father, but if he hangs around with prostitutes, his wealth is wasted.

Proverbs 26:11 As a dog returns to its vomit, so a fool repeats his folly.

2 Timothy 2:22 Run from anything that simulates youthful lust. Follow anything that makes you want to do right. Pursue faith, love and peace, and enjoy the companionship of those who call on the Lord with pure hearts.

Romans 6:1-23 (1) Well then, should we keep on sinning so that God can show us more and more of his wonderful grace? (2) Of course not! Since we have died to sin, how can we continue to live in it? (3) Or have you forgotten that when we were joined with Christ Jesus in baptism, we joined him in his death? (4) For we died and were buried with Christ by baptism. And just as Christ was raised from the dead by the glorious power of the Father, now we also may live new lives. (5) Since we have been united with him in his death, we will also be raised to life as he was. (6) We know that our old sinful selves were crucified with Christ so that sin might lose its power in our lives. We are no longer slaves to sin. (7) For when we died with Christ we were set free from the power of sin. (8) And since we died with Christ, we know we will also live with him. (9) We are sure of this because Christ was raised from the dead, and he will never die again. Death no longer has any power over him. (10) When he died, he died once to break the power of sin. But now that he lives, he lives for the glory of God. (11) So you also should consider yourselves to be dead to the power of sin and alive to God through Christ Jesus. (12) Do not let sin control the way you live; do not give in to lustful desires. (13) Do not let any part of your body become a tool of wickedness to be used for sinning. Instead, give yourselves completely to God, since you have been given new life, but now you have new life. And use your whole body as a tool to do what is right for the glory of God. (14) Sin is no longer your master, for you no longer subject to the law which enslaves you to sin. Instead, you are free by God's grace. (15) So since God's grace has set us free from the law, does this mean we can go on sinning? Of course not! (16) Don't you realize that whatever you choose to obey becomes your master? You can choose sin, which leads to death, or you can choose to obey God and receive his approval. (17) Thank God! Once you were slaves of sin, but now have obeyed with all your heart the new teaching God has given you. (18) Now you are free from sin, your old master, and you have become slaves to your new master, righteousness. (19) I speak this way, using the illustration of slaves and masters, because it is easy to understand. Before, you let yourselves be slaves of impurity and lawlessness. Now you must choose to be slaves of righteousness so that you will become holy. (20) In those days, when you were slaves of sin, you weren't concerned with doing what was right. (21) And what was the result? It was not good, since now you are ashamed of the things you used to do, things that end in eternal doom. (22) But now you are free from the power of sin and have become slaves of God. Now you do those things that lead to holiness and result in eternal life. (23) For the wages of sin is death, but the free gift of God is eternal life through Christ Jesus our Lord.

Colossians 3:5-11 (5) So put to death the sinful, earthly things lurking within you. Have nothing to do with sexual sin, impurity, lust and shameful desires. Anger will come upon those who do such things. (7) You use to do them when your life was part of this world. (8) But now is the time to get rid of anger, rage, malicious behavior, slander, and dirty language. (9) Don't lie to each other, for you have striped off your own evil nature and all it's wicked deeds. (10) In it's place you have "clothed yourselves with a brand new nature" that is continually being renewed as you learn more and more about Christ, who created this new nature within you. (11) In this new life, it doesn't matter if you are a Jew or a Gentile, circumcised or uncircumcised, barbaric, uncivilized, slave or free. Christ is all that matters, and he lives in all of us.

Ephesians 5:1-17 (1) Follow God's example in everything you do, because you are his dear children. (2) Live a life filled with love for others, following the example of Christ, who loved you and gave himself as a sacrifice to take away your sins. And God was pleased, because that sacrifice was like sweet perfume to him. (3) Let there be no sexual immorality, impurity, or greed among you. Such sins have no place among God's people. (4) Obscene stories, foolish talk, and coarse jokes, these are not for you. Instead let there be thankfulness to God. (5) You can be sure that no immoral, impure or greedy person will inherit the Kingdom of Christ and of God. For a greedy person is really an idolater who worships the things of this world. (6) don't be fooled by those who try to excuse their sins, for the terrible anger of God comes upon all those who disobey him. (7) Don't participate in the things these people do. (8) For though your hearts were once full of darkness, now you are full of light from the Lord. And your behavior should show it. (9) For this light within you produces only what is good and right and true. (10) Try to find out what is pleasing to the Lord. (11) Take no part in the worthless deeds of evil and darkness; instead, rebuke and expose them. (12) It is shameful even to talk about the things that unGodly people do in secret. (13) But when the light shines on them, it becomes clear how evil these things are. (14) And where your light shines, it will expose their evil deeds. That is why it is said, "Awake, O sleeper, rise up from the dead, and Christ will give you light." (15) So be careful how you live, not as fools, but as those who are wise. (16) Make the most for doing good in these evil days. (17) Don't act thoughtlessly, but try to understand what the Lord wants you to do.

Acts 2:38-39 (38) "Each of you must turn from your sins and turn to God, and be baptized in the name of Jesus Christ for the forgiveness of your sins. Then you will receive the gift of the Holy Spirit." (39) This promise is to you and your children, and even to the Gentiles, all who have been called to the Lord our God.

Galatians 5:16-25 (16) "So I advise you to live according to your new life in the Holy Spirit. Then you won't be doing what your sinful nature craves. (17) The old sinful nature loves to do evil, which is just the opposite from what the Holy Spirit wants. And the Spirit gives us desires which are the opposite from what the sinful nature desires. These forces are constantly fighting each other, and your choices are never free from this conflict. (18) But when you are directed by the Holy

Spirit, you are no longer subject to the law. (19) When you follow the desires of your sinful nature, your lives will produce these evil results: sexual immorality, impure thoughts, eagerness for lustful pleasures (20) idolatry, participation in demonic activities, hostility, quarreling, jealousy, outbursts of anger, selfish ambition, divisions, the feeling that everyone is wrong except those in your own little group, (21) envy, drunkenness, wild parties, and other kinds of sin. Let me tell you again, as I have before, that anyone living that sort of life will not inherit the Kingdom of God. (22) But when the Holy Spirit controls our lives, he will produce this kind of fruit in us: love, joy, peace, patience, kindness, goodness, faithfulness, (23) gentleness and self–control. Here there is no conflict with the law. (24) Those who belong to Christ Jesus, have nailed their passions and desires of their sinful natures to his cross and crucified them there. (25) If we are now living by the Holy Spirit, let us follow the Holy Spirit's leading in every part of our lives.

Romans 12:2 Do not conform any longer to the pattern of this world, but be transformed by the renewing of your mind. Then you will be able to test and approve what God's will is, his good pleasing and perfect will. (NIV)

Proverbs 4:5-6 Get wisdom, get understanding, do not forget my words or swerve from them. (6) Do not forsake wisdom, and she will protect you, love her and she will watch over you. (NIV)

Proverbs 4:14-15 Do not set foot on the path of the wicked or walk in the way of evil men. (15) Avoid it, do not travel on it, turn from it and go on your way. (NIV)

Psalms 26:1-5 Vindicate me, O Lord, for I have led a blameless life. I have trusted in the Lord without wavering, test me and try me, examine my heart and my mind, for your love is ever before me and I walk continually in your truth. I do not sit with deceitful men, nor do I consort with hypocrites, I abhor the assembly of evildoers and refuse to sit with the wicked.

1 Peter 5:8-9 Be careful! Watch out for attacks from the Devil, your great enemy. He prowls around like a roaring lion, looking for some victim to devour. (9) Take a firm stand against him and be strong in your faith. Remember that your Christian brothers and sisters all over the world are going through the same kind of suffering you are.

Proverbs 4:23,25-27 Above all else, guard your heart, for it is the wellspring of life. (25) Let your eyes look straight ahead, fix your gaze directly before you. (26) Make level paths for your feet and take only ways that are firm. (27) Do not swerve to the right or to the left, keep your foot from evil.

Proverbs 10:23 A fool finds pleasure in evil conduct, but a man of understanding delights in wisdom.

1 Corinthians 13:11 ...When I was a child, I spoke and thought and reasoned as a child does. But when I grew up, I put away childish things.

James 4:17 Remember, it is sin to know what you ought to do and then not do it.

Psalms 103:2 Praise the Lord, I tell myself, and never forget the good things he does for me.

Study Application Notes

Psalms 51:5-9 If we fail to admit our sin, it will continue to burden us with destructive guilt. We need to learn to confess and repent of our sin. Then we need to seek God's wisdom as to how we can make amends with the people we have wronged. Seeking forgiveness is essential for spiritual growth, and we can be sure that God will forgive us when we humbly come to him.

51:10-13 This Psalm of repentance was written by David after he committed adultery with Bathsheba and then arranged for her husband's death (2 Samuel 11-12). Why did God forgive David and offer him restoration? David was humble and repentant about his sin. He admitted it and asked for God's help and forgiveness. If we confess our sin and humbly seek God's forgiveness, there is hope for us, no matter how great our failures in the past.

51:10 Because we are born sinners (51:5) our natural inclination is to please ourselves rather than with God. David followed that inclination when he took another man's wife. We also follow it when we sin in any way. Like David, we must ask God to cleanse us from within (51:7), clearing our hearts and spirits for new thoughts and desires. Right conduct can only come from a clean heart and spirit. Ask God to create a pure heart and spirit in you. (NIV)

51:10 When God forgives our sin and restores us to a relationship with him, we want to reach out to others who need this forgiveness and reconciliation. The more you have felt God's forgiveness, the more you will desire to tell others about it. (NIV)

51:16-17 David realized that no number of sacrifices would cover his sin if he weren't sorry for what he had done. He knew that God would grant forgiveness to him if he honestly admitted his failures. We don't have to earn forgiveness from God. He graciously grants it when we repent and confess our sins. God desires true, heartfelt repentance rather than mere gestures or rituals. He is looking for us to take responsibility for our sins and humbly seek Gods forgiveness. God is looking for people with humble hearts, not perfect records.

Luke 18:10-14 The Pharisee in these verses did not have an accurate self-perception. He looked upon himself as better than others, his pride his ability to see himself or others as God did. He is a good example of what we are like when we refuse to see the truth. Most of us are guilty of ignoring our own sins by pointing a hypocritical finger at someone worse off than we are. God sees the heart and will reward us (forgive us, heal us, aid us in spiritual growth) according to our humble faith. The tax collector in this story with humble and honest self-awareness was on his way to true spiritual renewal. The Pharisee was headed for spiritual disaster.

1 John 1:8-9 Careful and honest reflection on God's word and our lives normally leads to a consciousness of sin. In these verses we assume that if we confess our sins, we will experience the forgiveness and cleansing God has provided through the blood shed by his Son, Jesus Christ. True confession involves a commitment not to continue in sin. We wouldn't be genuinely confessing our sins to God if we planned to commit them again and just wanted temporary forgiveness. We should pray for strength to defeat temptation the next time we face it. The lesson is simple, Confession must precede cleansing.

Proverbs 28:13 This verse contains wisdom essential to our spiritual growth and transformation. We must honestly assess our mistakes, confess our wrongs to one another and to God, and strive to avoid such mistakes in the future.

28:13 It is human nature to hide our sins or overlook our mistakes. But it is hard to learn from a mistake you don't acknowledge making. And what good is a mistake if it doesn't teach us something? To learn from an error you need to admit it, confess it, analyze it, and make adjustments so that it doesn't happen again. Everyone makes mistakes, but only a fool repeats them. (NIV)

Proverbs 3:5-7 What a promise! God will direct us and crown our efforts with success if we put our trust in him rather than to try to do it on our own. Putting God first means turning our lives and wills over to him. Surrendering to his lordship is humbling, but he will bless us as a result.

3:5-6 We must trust God completely in every choice we make. We should not omit careful thinking or belittle our God-given ability to reason, but we should not trust our own ideas to the exclusion of all others. We must not be wise in our own eyes. We should always be willing to listen to and be corrected by God's Word and wise counselors. Bring your decisions to God in prayer, use the Bible as your guide then follow God's leading. He will make your paths straight by both guiding and protecting you. (NIV)

3:6 To receive God's guidance, said Solomon, we must acknowledge God in all our ways. This means turning every area of our lives over to him. Look at your values and priorities. What is important to you? In what areas have you not acknowledge him? In many areas of your life you may already acknowledge God, but it is in the areas where you attempt to restrict or ignore his influence that will cause you grief. Make God a vital part of everything you do, then he will guide you because you will be working to accomplish his purposes. (NIV)

Proverbs 4:5-6 If you want wisdom, you must decide to go after it. This will take resolve, a determination not to abandon the search once you begin no matter how difficult the road may become. This is not a once in a lifetime step, but a daily process of choosing between two paths, the wicked and the righteous. (NIV)

Proverbs 4:14-15 Even friends can make you fall. It is difficult for people to except that friends and acquaintances might be luring them to do wrong. Young people who want to be accepted would never want to confront or criticize a friend for wrong plans or actions. Many other people can't even see how their friend's actions could lead to trouble. While we should be accepting of others, we need a healthy skepticism about human behavior. When you feel yourself being influenced proceed with caution. Don't let your friends cause you to fall into sin. (NIV)

Ephesians 4:22-24 Throw off your old sinful nature and your former way of life, which is corrupted by lust and deception. **(23)** Instead, let the Spirit renew your thoughts and attitudes. **(24)** Put on your new nature, created to be like God—truly righteous and holy.

Proverbs 23: 17-19 Don't envy sinners, but always continue to fear the LORD. **(18)** You will be rewarded for this; your hope will not be disappointed. **(19)** My child, listen and be wise: Keep your heart on the right course.

Proverbs 28:9 If anyone turns a deaf ear to the law, even his prayers are detestable.

James 5:19-20 My dear brothers and sisters, if someone among you wanders away from the truth and is brought back, **(20)** you can be sure that whoever brings the sinner back will save that person from death and bring about the forgiveness of many sins.

Proverbs 4:23,25-27 Our heart, our feelings of love and desire dictates to a great extent how we live because we always find time to do what we enjoy. Solomon tells us to guard our hearts above all else, making sure that we concentrate on those desires that will keep us on the right paths. Make sure your affections push you in the right direction. Put boundaries on your desires, don't go after everything you see. Look straight ahead, keep your eyes fixed on your goal and don't get sidetracked on detours that lead to sin.

Proverbs 26:11 We almost invariably repeat the patterns of the past, our old problems revisit us again and again. It is easy to slip back into familiar sinful patterns. That is why we need to be diligent to preserve our spiritual gains.

2 Timothy 2:22 Paul's advice to Timothy is appropriate for us, too. We need to run from the places and situations that are likely to lead to temptation. We are to avoid spending time with people who will lead us to a fall. Do you have a recurring temptation that you find difficult to resist? Remove yourself physically from any situation that stimulates your desire to sin. Knowing when to run is as important in spiritual battle as knowing when and how to fight. Instead, we are to spend time with people who will support our spiritual growth. If we don't have friends or activities that support our spiritual growth, we need to get involved in a community of Godly and supportive people.

Romans 6:1-3 If God loves to forgive, why not sin to give him added opportunities to forgive us? We may not admit it, but we act on this principle all too often. Paul's response to our use of this excuse for sin is an emphatic no. Such an attitude presumes upon God's grace and makes light of the tremendous cost of our salvation. It is unthinkable that we would continue to allow sin to be our master when we have surrendered our lives to God.

Romans 6:2-11 Paul examined how we can receive new life through the death and resurrection of Jesus Christ. He traced the stages of Jesus' life (1) His earthly body that was subject to death; (2) his death, burial and resurrection; and (3) his resurrection body that was no longer under the power of death. Next, Paul showed how are own lives can be parallel to Jesus: (1) We began under the mastery of sin and death; (2) we identify with Jesus' death burial and resurrection; (3) we receive new lives free from the power of sin and death. God has the power to take people headed for destruction and set them on the road to new life.

Romans 6:4 In the church of Paul's day, immersion was the usual form of baptism, that is, new Christians were completely "buried" in water. They understood this form of baptism to symbolize the death and burial of the old way of life. Coming up out of the water symbolized resurrection to new life with Christ. If we think of our old, sinful life as dead and buried, we have a powerful motive to resist sin. We can consciously choose to treat the desires and temptations of the old nature as if they were dead. Then we can continue to enjoy our wonderful new life with Jesus. (NIV)

6:5 We can enjoy our new life in Christ because we are united with him in his death and resurrection life, we have unbroken fellowship with God and freedom from sin's hold on us. (NIV)

6:6 The power and penalty of sin died with Christ on the cross. Our "old self" our sinful nature, died once and for all, so we are freed from its power. Here, Paul emphasizes that we no longer live under sin's power. God does not take us out of the world or make us robots, we will still feel like sinning and sometimes we will sin. The difference is that before we were saved we were slaves to our sinful nature, but now we can choose to live for Christ. (NIV)

6:8 Because of Christ's death and resurrection, his followers need never fear death. That assurance frees us to enjoy fellowship with him and to do his will. This will affect all our activities, work, worship, play, Bible study, quiet times and times of caring for others. When you know that you don't have to fear death, you will experience a new vigor in life. (NIV)

6:12-14 Paul recognized that temptation would be an ongoing reality, so he gave us this warning, "Do not give in." The temptations we experience are the extensions of the sinful natures that exist in each of us. Though we cannot overcome our sinful natures alone, we can ask God to help us. We are to reckon our sinful natures as crucified with Christ. As we call on the Lord, we have access to the Holy Spirit, who will help us overcome the powerful temptations in our lives.

6:19-22 It is impossible to be neutral when dealing with the spiritual realm. We all have a master, either sin or God. Making sin our master may seem fun for a while, but it will only lead to a life that is painfully out of control. When we surrender our lives to God, we affirm that God is our master. This is the only way we can hope to experience restoration of our lives. At first God's way may look harder than the way of sin, but in time we will discover that God's way is the only way to a joyful and meaningful life.

Colossians 3:5 We should consider ourselves dead and unresponsive to sexual immorality, impurity, lust, evil desires, and greed. The warning in this verse is not against sex, but against sexual perversion. Where is the line between the two? The Bible everywhere celebrates heterosexual, monogamous marriage as the proper situation for sexual fulfillment. Christian men and women should be open to true love, and to sexual intimacy, within the commitment to lifelong fidelity. That is God's way. The rest is dangerous and futile. Stay away! Sexual sin and perversion will drain your energies and turn your heart away from God.

3:6 The "God's terrible anger" refers to God's judgment on these kinds of behavior, culminating with future and final punishment of evil. When tempted to sin, remember that you must one day stand before God.

3:9 Lying to one another disrupts unity by destroying trust. It tears down relationships and may lead to serious conflicts in a family or Church. So don't exaggerate statistics, pass on rumors or gossip or say things to build up your own image. Be committed to telling the truth.

3:10 What doe's it mean to "cloth yourself with a brand new nature"? It means that your conduct should match your faith. If you are a Christian, you should act like it. To be a good Christian means more than just making good resolutions and having good intentions; it means taking the right actions. This is a straightforward step that is as simple as putting on your cloths. You must rid yourself of all evil practices and immorality. Then you can commit yourself to what Christ teaches and wants you to do. If you have made such a commitment, are you remaining true to it? What old cloths do you need to strip off? Remember, this commitment is a lifelong process. It takes practice, ongoing review, patience and concentration to keep in line with God's will.

3:11 We should have no barriers of nationality, race, education level, social standing, wealth, gender, religion or power. Christ breaks down all barriers and accepts all people who come to him. Nothing should keep us from telling others about Christ or accepting into our fellowship any and all believers. Christians should be building bridges, not walls.

Ephesians 5:1-7 God wants us to follow his will for our lives. Some of us may wonder how we can know what God wants us to do. Here we see that God wants us to be like Jesus Christ. As we look at his life, we can see how God would like us to think and act. We are to love our enemies, just as Jesus did. We are to avoid sexual impurity, greed and obscene speech since they stand counter to the character of God. As difficult as imitating Christ may sound, anything is possible with God's powerful help.

5:8 As people who have light from the Lord, your actions should reflect your faith. You should live above reproach morally so that you will reflect God's goodness to others. (NIV)

5:10-14 It is important to avoid the "fruitless deeds of darkness" (any pleasure or activity that results in sin) but we must go even further. Paul instructs us to expose these deeds, because our silence may be interpreted as approval. God needs people who will take a stand for what is right. (NIV)

Acts 2:38-39 Peter's preaching lead the people to examine their lives and ask the Apostle what they should do. They readily recognized their need for salvation in Christ and went on to receive God's powerful help. Peter assured them that by turning from their sins and surrendering their lives to God, they would be forgiven and receive the powerful presence of the Holy Spirit. We can expect the same blessings if we bring our failures before God. His forgiveness of our sins will set us free from our bondage to sin. The presence of his Holy Spirit will give us power to persevere as we follow Christ. Then we can fully experience the transformation and blessing he longs to bring into our lives.

Acts 2:38-39 To repent means to turn from sin, changing the direction of your life from selfishness and rebellion against God's laws. At the same time you must turn to Christ, depending on him for forgiveness, mercy, guidance and purpose. We cannot save ourselves, only God can save us. Baptism identifies us with Christ and with the community of believers. It is a condition of discipleship and a sign of faith. (NIV)

Galatians 5:16-21 Very often, God's will for us stands in direct opposition to our natural desires. We must see this truth and be willing to turn away from following our selfish desires and redirect our course back to doing God's will as revealed in the Bible. Here we find a whole list of destructive behaviors that flow out of a self-centered life. When we turn our lives over to God, however, we allow his spirit to help us control the desires that lead us to sin. More and more God's desires become our desires.

5:16-21 These characteristics are a product of the Holy Spirit's work in a life submitted to God and his plan. Just as a tree bears fruit by means of God's silent work behind the scenes, we produce this fruit of the spirit by means of God's power alone. Our part is to surrender our lives to him. When the Holy Spirit begins to bear this fruit in our lives, sin loses its power. With joy and peace, we overcome the pain of our broken past. With love, kindness, goodness, faithfulness, and gentleness we restore our relationships and make restitution. With patience, we persevere through the difficult times. With self-control we stand against temptation. God's spirit can supply everything we need for fruitful lives.

Romans 12:2 We are called to "not to conform any longer to the pattern of this world", with its behavior and customs that are usually selfish and often corrupting. However our refusal must go even deeper than the level of behavior and customs, it must be firmly planted in our minds. "Be transformed by the renewing of your mind." Only when the Holy Spirit renews, reeducates and redirects our minds are we truly transformed. (NIV)

Ephesians 4:22-24 Our old way of life before we believed in Christ is completely in the past. This is both a once for all decision and a daily conscious commitment. We are not to be driven by desire and impulse. We must put on a new role, head in a new direction, and have the new way of thinking that the Holy Spirit gives.

Proverbs 28:9 God does not listen to our prayers if we intend to go back to our sins as soon as we get off our knees. What closes his ears is not the depth of our sin, but our secret intention of doing it again. God hears our intentions as clearly as he hears our words.

James 5:19-20 If we truly believe God's word we will live it day by day. God's Word is not merely something we read or think about but something we do. Belief, faith and trust must have hands and feet - ours!

Psalms 26:1-5 Should we stay away from unbelievers? No. There is a difference between being with unbelievers and being one of them. Consider the people you enjoy and if you are often with them, will you become less obedient to God in outlook and action. If yes, carefully monitor how you spend time with them.

1 Peter 5.8-9 Satan is lurking and prowling about in this world, seeking to devour us. We are commanded to stand firm and fight the battle, knowing that the war is already won. As we develop a community of support, we will see that we are not alone in the battle, others are fighting alongside us.

James 4:17 We tend to think that doing wrong is sin. But James tells us that sin is also not doing right. (These two kinds of sin are sometimes called sins of commission and sins of omission). It is a sin to lie, it can also be a sin to know the truth and not tell it. It is a sin to speak evil of someone; it can also be a sin to avoid him or her when you know that they need your friendship. We should be willing to help as the Holy Spirit guides us. If God has directed you to do a kind act, to render a service, or to restore a relationship, do it! You will experience a renewed and refreshed vitality to your Christian faith. (NIV)

Self Reflection

1. How does this topic apply to me?

2. What truths in this area can I recognize and how can I fully address them?

3. Which Bible verses here best encourage and inspire me to want to be a better husband, father and man in this area?

4. What steps can I begin to take today to strengthen myself in this area?

5. Who can I reach out to for personal help and support in this area? (This could be a family member, friend, professional counselor, a spiritual leader or someone you worship with)

Journal

Journal

Part III

Additional Resources

Retraining Your Eyes and Mind/Setting Up Your Defense Perimeter
Tools to help maintain sexual purity

A. Bouncing Your Eyes Strategy

1. Training your eyes to "bounce" away from sights of pretty woman and sensual images. Put in practice for six weeks in order to change habit.

   - Build reflex action to immediately bounce or quickly move your eyes away from any sexual image or object that is not your wife or committed partner.

2. Your Tactics

   - Study yourself and ask how and where you are attacked the most.
   - Define your defense for each of the greatest enemies you've identified.
   - List your most obvious and prolific sources of sensual images apart from your wife.

   - List where you are weakest. List five biggest areas.
   a.

   b.

   c.

   d.

   e.

3. Define Your Defenses, how and what specifically you will do to train your eyes to bounce away from the items on your list.

   a.

   b.

   c.

   d.

   e.

Starving The Eyes Strategy

1. *Starve our eyes from the "bowels" of sexual gratification that come from outside our marriage.*

   a. Go cold turkey on sexual images including those on TV, R-rated movies, magazines and books for a three-week period. This also includes engaging in looking emphatically at female's body parts (anatomy) that makes you crave sexual lust.

   b. Focus totally on drawing sexual gratification from your wife.

2. *The sexual payoff from following this strategy:*

   a. You will be in harmony with God's will and marriage instructions for you. He will provide joy, peace and trills to your sexual life.

   b. Focusing your full attention on "your fountain" will result in your wife becoming more beautiful and sexier to you.

   c. Your wife's strengths and weaknesses will become your taste and she will be beyond comparison.

3. *Your Sword and Shield*

   a. Find a good Bible verse to use as a sword and rallying point when aroused sexually by an image or object other than your wife.
      - Memorize a verse of scripture about purity
      - Verse should be short. Job 31:1 is suggested and reads:

      "I have made a covenant with my eyes." Say to yourself: I can't do that

   b. Find a good Bible verse to use as a shield.
      - Memorize a verse that you can reflect on and draw strength from.
      - 1 Corinthians 6:18-20 is a suggested scripture:

"Flee from sexual immorality... You are not your own: you were bought at a price. Therefore honor God with your body."

(This verse's practical translation is: You have no right to look at or think about it. You haven't the authority.)

- Repeat this as many times as needed when you are facing sensual images or thoughts.

c. Benefits

- Will help you think rightly about real issues involved as you face temptation in your fight for sexual purity.
- Your sword and shield will help strengthen you in controlling your eyes and mind.
- You are able to close the door on Satan's counsel.
- You are now letting God control your thoughts and actions.
- You now begin to live to please your wife!

Material from this outline comes from Every Man's Battle-Winning the War on Sexual Temptation One Victory at a Time tm. For more on this subject refer to Chapters 11, 12 & 13.

(Used with permission)

Deterring Immorality by Counting Its Cost
The exorbitant price of sexual sin by Randy Alcorn

In 1850 Nathaniel Hawthorne published The Scarlet Letter, a powerful novel centered around the adulterous relationship of Hester Prynne and the highly respected minister, Reverend Mr. Arthur Dimmesdale. The fallen pastor, remorseful but not ready to face the consequences, asks the question, "What can a ruined soul, like mine, effect towards the redemption of other souls? or a polluted soul, towards their purification?" He describes the misery of standing in his pulpit and seeing the admiration of his people, and having to "then look inward, and discern the black reality of what they idolize." Finally he says, "I have laughed, in bitterness and agony of heart, at the contrast between what I seem and what I am! And Satan laughs at it!"

Ruined, polluted, black reality, bitterness, and agony. And perhaps, worst of all, Satan's laugh. These are just some of the consequences of sexual immorality in the life of one known as a follower of God.

I met with a man who had been a leader in a Christian organization until he committed immorality. I asked him, "What could have been done to prevent this?" He paused only for a moment, then said with haunting pain and precision, "If only I had really known, really thought through and weighed what it would cost me and my family and my Lord, I honestly believe I would never have done it."

Some years ago my friend Alan Hlavka and I both developed lists of all the specific consequences we could think of that would result from our immorality as pastors. The lists were devastating, and to us they spoke more powerfully than any sermon or article on the subject.

Periodically, especially when traveling or when in a time of temptation or weakness, we read through this list. In a personal and tangible way it brings home God's inviolate law of choice and consequence. It cuts through the fog of rationalization and fills our hearts with the healthy, motivating fear of God. **We find that when we begin to think unclearly, reviewing this list yanks us back to the reality of the law of the harvest and the need both to fear God and the consequences of sin.**

An edited version of our combined lists follows. I've included the actual names of my wife and daughters to emphasize the personal nature of this exercise. Where it involves my own lists of specific people's names, I've simply stated "list names" so the reader can insert the appropriate ones in his own life.

Some of these consequences would be unique to me, just as some of yours would be unique to you. I recommend that you use this as the basis for your own list, then include those other consequences that would be uniquely yours. The idea, of course, is not to focus on sin, but on the consequences of sin, thereby encouraging us to refocus on the Lord and take steps of wisdom and purity that can keep us from falling. (While God can forgive and bring beauty out of ashes, that's a message to those who have already sinned...not to those who are contemplating sin! On the "front side" of sin we must not give assurances of forgiveness and restoration. We must put the focus where Scripture does on the love of God and the fear of God, both of which should act in concert to motivate us to holy obedience.)

Personalized List of Anticipated Consequences of Immorality
By Pastor Randy Alcorn

1. Grieving my Lord; displeasing the One whose opinion most matters.
2. Dragging into the mud Christ's sacred reputation.
3. Loss of reward and commendation from God.
4. Having to one day look Jesus in the face at the judgment seat and give an account of why I did it.
5. Forcing God to discipline me in various ways.
6. Following in the footsteps of men I know of whose immorality forfeited their ministry and caused me to shudder. List of these names:
7. Suffering of innocent people around me who would get hit by my shrapnel (a la Achan).
8. Untold hurt to Nanci, my best friend and loyal wife.
9. Loss of Nanci's respect and trust.
10. Hurt to and loss of credibility with my beloved daughters, Karina and Angela. ("Why listen to a man who betrayed Mom and us?")
11. If my blindness should continue or my family be unable to forgive, I could lose my wife and my children forever.
12. Shame to my family. ("Why isn't Daddy a pastor anymore?"; the cruel comments of others who would invariably find out.)
13. Shame to my church family.
14. Shame and hurt to my fellow pastors and elders. List of names:
15. Shame and hurt to my friends, and especially those I've led to Christ and discipled. List of names:
16. Guilt awfully hard to shake—even though God would forgive me, would I forgive myself?
17. Plaguing memories and flashbacks that could taint future intimacy with my wife.
18. Disqualifying myself after having preached to others.
19. Surrender of the things I am called to and love to do, teach and preach and write and minister to others. Forfeiting forever certain opportunities to serve God. Years of training and experience in ministry wasted for a long period of time, maybe permanently.
20. Being haunted by my sin as I look in the eyes of others, and having it all dredged up again wherever I go and whatever I do.

21. Undermining the hard work and prayers of others by saying to our community "this is a hypocrite, who can take seriously anything he and his church have said and done?"

22. Laughter, rejoicing and blasphemous smugness by those who disrespect God and the church. (2 Samuel 12:14).

23. Bringing great pleasure to Satan, the Enemy of God.

24. Heaping judgment and endless problems on the person I would have committed adultery with.

25. Possible diseases: gonorrhea, syphilis, chlamydia, herpes, and AIDS (pain, constant reminder to me and my wife, possible infection of Nanci, or in the case of AIDS, even causing her death, as well as mine.)

26. Possible pregnancy, with its personal and financial implications, including a lifelong reminder of sin to my family and me.

27. Loss of self-respect, discrediting my own name, and invoking shame and lifelong embarrassment upon myself.

These are only some of the consequences. **If only we would rehearse in advance the ugly and overwhelming consequences of immorality, we would be far more prone to avoid it.** May we live each day in the love and fear of God.

Manformation Creed

Our motto is: I AIM HI... *I Am Intentionally Modeling His Image*

The Manformation Project is a faith-based group mentoring and rites of passage setting that brings together 10-18 year old boys with Godly men in a safe fun environment to encourage, support & cultivate positive growth. Their mission is to create an experience for boys that nurtures and affirms their identity as a son of God. At the same time, they offer life skills and goal setting discussions with practical tools and information to help urban boys mature into fruitful men, free from the criminal justice system. (website: www.manformation.org/1.html)

Principles Of Manhood

A man's source of strength is God
A man must be as strong as possible – mentally and physically
A man must protect his loved ones, even to his death
A man must provide for his family
A man's word is his bond
A man must have discipline
A man must have the will to win
A man knows that the will to win means nothing without the will to prepare
A man must know the difference between right and wrong
A man must be willing to take the consequences of his actions
A man must not misuse his strength
A man helps those who are good, yet weaker than he
A man must have a plan
A man will know fear but must still must function
A man will always do his best
A man must be able to take the bitter as well as the sweet
A man must have priorities
A man knows there are many times he must stand alone
A man must be willing to take a calculated risk
A man must know his strengths and weaknesses
A man must use his wisdom and understanding
A man must know that before he can lead he must follow
A man knows, when in doubt to ask God.

~ By: Ronald M. Barnes

(Used with permission)

Five Things I Wish I'd Known Before Marriage by Dave Boehi

1. Marriage is not all about you, it's not about your happiness and self-fulfillment. It's not about getting your needs met. It's about going through life together and serving God together and serving each other.

2. You are about to learn a painful lesson, you are both very selfish people. This may be very difficult to comprehend during the happy and haze days of courtship. But it's true and it shocks many couples during their first years of marriage.

3. The person you love the most is also the person who can hurt you the deepest. That's the risk and pain of marriage. And the beauty of marriage is working through your hurt and pain and resolving your conflicts and solving your problems.

4. You can't make it work on your own. It's obvious that marriage is difficult, just look at how many couples today end up in divorce. To make your marriage last for a lifetime, you need to rely on God for the power and love and strength and wisdom and endurance you need.

5. Never stop enjoying each other. Always remember that marriage is an incredible gift to be enjoyed. *Ecclesiastes 9:9* says, *"Enjoy life with your wife, whom you love, all the days of this meaningless life that God has given you under the sun— all your meaningless days. For this is your lot in life and in your toilsome labor under the sun."*

(Used with permission)

Christian Family Pledge
By Pastor Dudley Rutherford

1. Each day I will spend at least as much time with my child as I do with my TV.

2. Each day I will share at least one fun-filled learning experience with my child.

3. Each day I will affirm my child as a person.

4. Each day I will affirm my Lord (praise Him, thank Him, honor Him) in the presence of my child.

5. Each day I will affirm my mate in the presence of my child.

6. Each day I will say, "I love you" to my child.

7. Each day I will make one truth from God's Word the delight of my child's life.

8. Each day I will pray for my child by name.

9. Each day I will read something to my child that will build his/her love for the Lord and the joy of reading.

10. Each day I will help my child feel the warmth of my personal presence by an embrace, a hug or a kiss.

(Used with permission)

Father's Day Letter To My Children

June 21, 2010

Dear Jason and Dominique,

Thank you both for your Father's Day greetings, your love, thoughtfulness and respect. My love for both of you knows no end and in truth you show me "Father's Day Love" on an ongoing basis. Father's Day has now taken on a new meaning for me, it is no longer a day to receive but a day to reflect on doing the following:

1. How I can be a better father to each of you in the coming year.

2. How I can be a more dependable father to you.

3. How I can work on being more available to each of you and your needs in the coming year.

4. How I can better be the father that you two will look up to and be proud to call dad.

5. How I can be a better husband to your mom, who is the greatest woman in the world!

6. To use the day to connect with other special men in my life who are fathers. To let them know that I treasure their friendship and bond.

7. To thank God for choosing me to be your father and to know how blessed I am to have you Jason and Dominique as my children!

Love Dad

Postlude

Father's Day Letter From My Son

June 19, 2011

Happy Father's Day!
Looking forward to another
year with "The virtuous Man"
as my dad.

love,
Jason
and
Tiffany

New Marching Orders

"Forget the former things;
do not dwell on the past.
See, I am doing a new thing!
Now it springs up; do you not perceive it?
I am making a way in the wilderness
and streams in the wasteland.

Isaiah 43:18-19 (NIV)

About The Author

An award winning two time Grammy™ nominated pianist, composer, arranger, producer, educator and author, Kevin Toney first started playing piano at age five in his city of birth, Detroit, Michigan. At age eight, he added cello and alto saxophone to his skill set. He later attended the prestigious Cass Technical High School and performed with many of his city's top musicians. Kevin graduated to attend Howard University in Washington, D.C. where he earned his B.A. in composition and jazz studies. During his tenure, he became the leader of the The Blackbyrds, the innovative jazz-r&b fusion sextet founded by jazz trumpet legend Donald Byrd. Kevin wrote and co-penned many of the band's most memorable music including "Rock Creek Park", "All I Ask," and the Grammy-nominated scorcher "Unfinished Business." After six '70s Soul classics, Kevin left the group and recorded his first solo LP, *Special K* in 1982.

Kevin Toney truly came into his own with his 1994 release *Lovescape*, featuring his composition "Kings" which became a staple of then burgeoning smooth jazz radio. Over the next decade-plus, Kevin's sound evolved over seven more meticulously crafted CDs that found him experimenting in nearly every contemporary music palette. Among the honors he earned was having his 2001 album *Strut* selected by the 2002 Winter Olympics Committee as "official music" alongside that of Paul McCartney and Alicia Keys. Kevin's latest release is "New American Suite" which introduces his amazing new trio, The Kevin Toney 3.

Beyond his own music, Kevin has performed with an impressive survey of major artists that includes Aretha Franklin, Stevie Wonder, Shania Twain, Isaac Hayes, Carl Anderson, Shirley Caesar, Oscar Brown Jr., Edwin Hawkins, Pink, Kenny Burrell, Whitney Houston, Norman Brown, Peter White and more. He also scored two films: the period drama "Kings of the Evening" (starring Lynn Whitfield and Tyson Beckford) and the documentary "The Kinsey Collection" (about a married couple that assembled the largest collection of African and African American artifacts in the United States).

Kevin's musical accompaniment to The Virtuous Man book is a CD titled *"Heart of Gratitude"* (a.k.a. *A Grateful Heart*). This solo piano recording takes the listener on a spiritual journey through music in hopes of encouraging a deeper connection with God. Mirroring the message of that music, Kevin is a mentor for the 'Manformation Project,' a Los Angeles-based rites of passage setting that brings boys of 10-18 years of age into contact with Godly minded men to cultivate positive growth. Kevin and his wife – Phyllis – also started *The Toney Family Foundation*, focusing on arts and music related philanthropy.

But most importantly, spirit has been calling Kevin higher in recent years. Beginning in 1990 when he was invited by the renowned Rev. Dr. O.C. Smith to bring his music to The City Of Angels Church in Los Angeles, California. He has since answered the call of God and the Holy Spirit playing his music in diverse spiritual centers including Agape International Spiritual Center, Saddleback Church and TBN's "Praise The Lord". Kevin loves to cook, read the Bible and enjoys walking, but his greatest love is the Lord, his wife and children.

Products by Kevin Toney

Books
The Virtuous Man (softcover and ebook)
A Heart of Gratitude Songbook
The Kevin Toney Collection Volume 1
New American Suite Collection

Recordings

New American Suite	2012 KTE
Kings Of The Evening (Soundtrack)	2011 KTE/PPF
A Heart Of Gratitude (aka A Grateful Heart)	2008 KTE
Retrospectives	2006 DM
110 Degrees And Rising	2005 Shanachie
Sweet Spot	2003 Shanachie
Strut	2001 Shanachie
Satin Doll	2000 Shanachie
Extra Sensual Perception	1999 Shanachie
Pastel Mood	1995 Ichiban
Lovescape	1994 Ichiban
Special K	1982 Fantasy

Sheet Music
Includes individual leadsheet, piano music, small combo and big band scores.

Contact Information
Kevin Toney is available to come speak and perform at your men's group, young men's organizations, marriage related events, conferences, seminars, workshops and special events.

To schedule an event contact:

Virtuous Man Ministries
c/o K-Tone Enterprises
19360 Rinaldi Street, Suite 476
Porter Ranch, California 91326
Tel; 818-623-7081
email: teamtoney4@gmail.com
website: www.kevintoney.com for more information

CPSIA information can be obtained at www.ICGtesting.com
Printed in the USA
LVOW07s0251111213

364811LV00010B/212/P